Night Moves

Also by Don Breithaupt and Jeff Breithaupt

Precious and Few: Pop Music in the Early '70s

DON BREITHAUPT AND
JEFF BREITHAUPT

FOREWORD BY JOE JACKSON

Night
Moves

POP MUSIC IN THE LATE '70S

St. Martin's Griffin ✹ New York

www.stmartins.com

Book design by Clair Moritz

Introductory quote © Leonard Cohen. Originally printed in *Death of a Lady's Man,* 1978. Used by permission/All rights reserved. Permission also granted by McClelland & Stewart, Inc., the Canadian publishers.

Library of Congress Cataloging-in-Publication Data

Breithaupt, Don.
    Night moves : pop music in the late '70s / Don Breithaupt and Jeff Breithaupt.
        p.   cm.
    Includes index.
    ISBN 0-312-19821-3
        1. Popular music—1971–1980—History and criticism.   I. Breithaupt, Jeff. II. Title.
ML3470 .B739 2000
781.64'0973—dc21   00-024292

First edition: July 2000

10 9 8 7 6 5 4 3 2 1

For Rikki and the boys, my deeper music

—D.B.

For Shelley and her big, beautiful spirit

—J.B.

Contents

Acknowledgments

Thanks to Mom and Dad for everything, but especially for relinquishing control of the car radio for an entire decade; Ross, this endeavor's silent partner; Shelley and Rikki for their love and support (and input); Marian Lizzi for her patience, enthusiasm, and insightful edits; Joe Jackson; Clair Moritz; Donald Lehr; Dave Donald; Paul Kellogg; Miss Walton; Joel Whitburn; BPI Communications, Inc.; NARAS; the record labels.

Put on the radio. Light up a cigarette. You are a normal citizen. Fiddle among the stations. Find a good tune.

—Leonard Cohen
Death of a Lady's Man, 1978

Foreword

THE LATE SEVENTIES
Joe Jackson

I hate nostalgia.

In my early teens, I rolled my eyes as my mother sighed over the lack of dance-halls in our home town. Why, there were dozens before the war; Hitler's bombers blasted most of them to bits and the ones that were left turned into bingo parlors or worse. What did I care? I was a Beethoven fanatic.

By my late teens, I was a Bowie fanatic, and people in their thirties sneered. Rock'n'roll, the *real* rock'n'roll, was already dead for them. It died along with that magical decade, the sixties, and the seventies was a musical wasteland. I rolled my eyes again.

Much more recently, I've had arguments with people who think that electronic dance music is not music at all. The *real* music, they say, was back in the seventies, when people had to play real instruments. Guitars, for instance, even though most of the spiky-haired upstarts you saw in punk bands at the time barely knew how to strap them on and plug them in, let alone tune them up. I seem to remember a few arguments about that, too.

Please, God, let no one's eyes roll when I talk about the past. I'm really more interested in Right Now, which for all I know might be a Golden Age—it's hard to judge when you're in the middle of it. Chance distributes talent unevenly, creating the impression of peaks and troughs. From a more objective distance, though, every musical epoch seems to contain about the same proportion of the good, the bad, and the yawningly mediocre.

So I'm not going to claim that the late seventies were *better* than now. In a lot of ways they were worse. A shaky economy, high unemployment, racial unrest, and we didn't even have e-mail. Instead I'll have to talk about how they were *different*.

It was an edgy, exciting time. The pace of musical change was accelerating, although new styles still took a bit longer to catch on than they do now. They still erupted on the street and worked their way upwards, established themselves a bit before they had a chance to be bastardized and exploited. Now, at the turn of the century, acceleration is a constant, and there's no *resistance*. Someone invents a new beat, a new sound, and the following week, you hear it in a car commercial.

In the late seventies there was still enough resistance for the Sex Pistols to be truly shocking. Anarchists who weren't so much creating music as doing their damnedest to actually *destroy* it. A kind of upside-down logic comes into play here: the Pistols ultimately failed because they succeeded. "God Save the Queen" went to Number One despite being banned by the BBC—and one thing you can always bet on is that if something is profitable, the entertainment industry will find a way to absorb it. And if the Sex Pistols could be absorbed, then *anything* could. Hence another kind of nostalgia, for a time when being rebellious was actually rebellious. Or perhaps that's really nostalgia for being rebellious *in a certain way*.

I was in my early twenties when all this happened. And being in my early twenties, and having just moved to London, I was caught up in it all in a way that I might not have been if I'd been born, say, ten years earlier. In London in 1977, you could have found me most weeks at a frantic, sweaty club called the Vortex. I saw bands there whose names we've all forgotten, thrashing their instruments almost to pieces, while the crowd smashed and slammed and jerked each other up and down with chains or dog collars. And spat, too. "Gobbing" at the

performers was all part of the fun, or all part of some nihilis-
tic hate ritual—I was never quite sure which. As I watched
one band, the singer opened his mouth wide and, just as he let
out a blood-curdling scream, a thick gob of phlegm sailed
right into the back of his throat. He spent the next five minutes assaulting nearby members of the audience with his
mike stand—it must have been one of you bastards!—as the
spit kept coming. I wonder what happened to that guy. He
never achieved immortality as a glamorous junkie suicide, but
he probably had a dose of hepatitis to be proud of.

But I'm getting carried away here: Punk was not the only
thing happening in the late seventies, just the most colorful.
We're all guilty of categorizing eras and genres in simplistic
ways. We don't have time for the messy reality, which in the case
of the late seventies in the U.K., was that you could do pretty
much anything you wanted as long as you didn't wear *flares*. In
the United States, even that stricture didn't seem to apply.
Nineteen seventy-seven was the year of the Ramones, but also
the year of Foreigner, Styx, the Commodores, and Donna Summer. As the Pistols excoriated the Queen's "fascist regime,"
Crystal Gayle pleaded with someone not to make her brown
eyes blue, and Joe Tex vowed never to "bump no more with no
big fat woman."

Despite this dizzying variety, things were, in some ways,
simpler. No Internet, no computer games, no MTV, no DVD,
just records and gigs. But they seemed *really* important, and
not only because we had fewer distractions. Rivalries were
fiercer then, too, and short hair versus long was not just a
fashion footnote but a major tribal distinction. Older rockers
snarled at younger ones, like recently empowered eighteen-
year-olds who'd rather die than play with their little brothers.
But rockers of all ages lined up against R&B and dance music.
On my first American tour, in 1979, people kept giving me

buttons that said DISCO SUCKS. I didn't have the heart to tell them that I actually rather liked it.

I was touring, of course, because my first album—recorded in the summer of 1978—had finally been released. I was the right age in the right place at the right time, and I was inflamed enough by the so-called New Wave to tailor my music at least superficially to the zeitgeist. Basically this meant stripping it down to just guitar, bass and drums, and keeping it as simple as possible. More sophisticated ideas would have to wait till later. Now it can be revealed: I was a graduate of the Royal Academy of Music, but I tried very hard to keep that a *secret*.

On that same first tour, we played homemade tapes of obscure heavy reggae in between sets. Reggae was cool in London. Naive and arrogant, we wanted to educate the Yanks, who were only just starting to notice Bob Marley.

By 1980, bands like Madness and the Specials were reinventing ska. Genres and subgenres were multiplying like hyperactive amoebas. In retrospect, the late seventies looks more than anything else like a time of fragmentation. The style wars were so passionate and bewildering that it would have been hard, then, to imagine anyone tackling it all in one book. But here you are holding that book in your hand, and within its pages, the Clash are at last united with Meat Loaf, Chic, and the Village People by the only force that could ever have united them: chronology.

The late seventies created a musical climate in which anything could happen next . . . and didn't. The eighties by comparison, seemed dull. The nineties were much more interesting. But that's just my opinion, and we've probably had enough of that for now.

Enjoy this little vacation in the musical past. Just try not to get *stuck* there.

Introduction

When the nostalgic go searching for the late 1970s' heart of darkness, they might imagine that the compound at the end of the river will be crawling with blow-dried discophiles and peroxide punkers. Picture a world of both polyester and safety pins, Harvey Wallbangers and heroin, where a Carter-era Colonel Kurtz leads his followers in prayer: "Boogie oogie oogie—bollocks!"

The truth is at once more mundane and more complicated. Though punk and disco do represent the extremes of the late-seventies popular culture, they are hardly its heart. For that we need to revisit platinum-selling megastars like the Eagles, Fleetwood Mac, ABBA, Peter Frampton, and the Bee Gees. The era's bona fide creative movements grew out of a few grimy nightclubs in New York and London, but its commercial center was the football stadiums of middle America.

The late seventies, after all, were about nothing if not bigness. From the Concorde to the Howard Hughes estate, from Bigfoot to *Roots*, the world was attuned to the concept of being first, biggest, best. In the music business, words like "event," "blockbuster," and "multiplatinum" were bandied about freely, as though there were no tomorrow (there was, and its name was MTV). Sales records were broken and rebroken as pop touchstones (*Hotel California, Rumours, Minute by Minute*), future classic-rock staples (*Bat Out of Hell, Boston, Frampton Comes Alive!*), and slick movie soundtracks (*Saturday Night Fever, Grease, A Star Is Born*) reasserted the commercial supremacy of white American pop, and the concert business expanded to match. Dickey

Lee's "9,999,999 Tears" (1976) exponentially one-upped ?
[Question Mark] and the Mysterians' hit "96 Tears" (1966).
The Bee Gees notched seven number-one singles—seven
more than elite songwriters like Bruce Springsteen, Kate
Bush, Neil Young, and Elvis Costello could manage. Parallel-
ing the path of post–*Star Wars* cinema, the music industry
became an impersonal machine feeding on its own obscene
success, constantly hungering for the next big thing. (These
days, we take eight-figure sales reports for granted, but in the
late seventies, ten million albums was still *very* big news.)

Sometime around 1976, the archetypal early-seventies
rock fan, a bell-bottomed pothead praying for a Beatles reunion, morphed into the archetypal *late*-seventies rock fan: a
straight-legged pothead wearing a KISS Army T-shirt. The two
styles were as different as Paul McCartney and Paul Stanley.
From 1971 to 1975, mainstream rock had been resolutely post-
sixties—everything from Three Dog Night to Led Zeppelin had
a "none of this would have been possible without the Beatles"
subtext—but after 1976, the genre reinvented itself in the image of a Big Mac. Rock's blues roots disappeared in a din of
meticulously arranged lead-guitar lines and toothless power
chords. The trappings of stardom now included Lear jets, personal "pharmacists," and vanity labels. Faceless, spit-polished
anti-bands like Styx, Foreigner, and Journey became like fran-
chises of the same multinational fast-food chain—whether you
were in Boston or Kansas, the Meat Loaf tasted the same. The
Grand Illusion was that this was rock at all.

If corporate rock fostered less brand loyalty than previous
styles had, it didn't bother the record companies, whose profits were soaring (they peaked in 1978)—why worry about
the lightning-fast rise and fall of an act like Peter Frampton
when there seemed to be an endless supply of singing heads
coming down the pipeline right behind him? For the first

time, rock fans became aware that they were a "market," as opposed to, say, a "new generation."

The first casualty of the biz's newfound financial savvy was the strong personal bond between performer and audience that had been almost palpable in the heady days of Beatlemania. NASA's *Voyager* and *Pioneer* probes were successfully exploring the solar system's "icy giants," but no one could pierce the cold exterior of most terrestrial pop idols. It was the age of the acronym, with ABBA, ARS, AWB, BTO, ELO, ELP, LTD, M, Q, and X among the decade's hitmakers (calling the Atlanta Rhythm Section "ARS" is like calling Christmas Day "12/25"). Even as political leaders were making themselves more accessible—Jimmy Carter began fielding calls on radio in 1977—pop stars were growing more remote.

In this climate, disco was the perfect product. It was formulaic as no pop genre had ever been. It didn't require hard-to-manufacture attributes like personality, narrative voice, attitude, or vision. And, since the disco fan was a creature ruled by highly perishable trends, an endless stream of "new" product was essential. Disco's auteurs weren't trailblazers like John Lennon, Bob Dylan, or Brian Wilson, but technocrats like Giorgio Moroder, Nile Rodgers, and Harry Wayne Casey (known to the world as "K.C.").

Unless you were a rackjobber, calling music "product" would have seemed unthinkable even five years earlier. But what else could you call K.C. and the Sunshine Band's string of shockingly self-referential hits? Or the calculated disco contributions of legends like the Rolling Stones ("Miss You"), Barbra Streisand ("No More Tears [Enough Is Enough]"), and Rod Stewart ("Da Ya Think I'm Sexy?")? Disco, the music industry's great off-white hope, *was* a product. Like a corporate giant absorbing smaller companies, it swallowed established black-music strongholds like Philly soul and Motown whole.

The rise of disco paralleled the growth of the so-called "cult of self," in which the one-for-all ethos of the sixties ("Get Together") was abandoned in favor of a new, hedonistic code of conduct ("Get Down"). The battle of the sexes, the rape of the environment, and the cynical conduct of the former Nixon administration (it was a rare Watergate player who *didn't* pen a tell-all) continued unabated, but these things no longer captured the imagination of the young—like the record labels they so generously subsidized, young people were "looking out for number one."

Our own experience of this strange time included at least one communal moment. At four-thirty on a pitiless weekday winter morning in 1977, we, along with some like-minded friends, rode our ten-speeds to Marmac Jewelers, a humble establishment in a local plaza. When we arrived, the lineup had already started: headbangers, teenyboppers, overage biker-types, and progressive-rock fans (our camp) alike had come to buy Supertramp tickets. In those days, a printer would print the entire run of tickets for an event and distribute them to outlets big and small, so if you could find a lesser known dealer like Marmac, you could get great seats. Or so the theory went. This day, it appeared the secret was out, because the crowd was growing hourly.

As the sun rose, toughs stole loaves of bread from flats behind the grocery store, police drove by at intervals, and the whole group (well, okay, not the police) broke into spontaneous choruses of Supertramp chestnuts like "Dreamer" and "Bloody Well Right." For once, we weren't marooned on separate desert islands, staking out our highly specific musical territory. We were huddled together, freezing our asses off, singing the same song. It was, we guessed—we hoped—kind of like the sixties.

Meanwhile, amid a strange mixture of darkness and frivolity

(Jim Jones's Guyana, Ricardo Montalban's *Fantasy Island* TV series), some of the most ambitious, engaging, intelligent, and downright *musical* pop music of the century was being handmade by such old-world artisans as Paul Simon, Rickie Lee Jones, Randy Newman, Joni Mitchell, James Taylor, David Bowie, Elvis Costello, Todd Rundgren, and the Rodgers and Hart of alienation, Walter Becker and Donald Fagen. In fact, faced with pop masterpieces like *Aja, Station to Station, Hejira,* and *Little Criminals,* it's easy to think of the late seventies as an underappreciated golden age.

Then you remember that "You Light Up My Life" was the era's biggest hit. Sure, John Denver, Tony Orlando, and the Carpenters dropped out of sight, but nouveau-softies like Debby Boone, Leo Sayer, and Andy Gibb filled the void. Pop music began to streamline itself, throwing its corporate heft behind glossy behemoths like *Grease,* while marginalizing offbeat geniuses like David Byrne. The album overtook the less profitable 7-inch single as the dominant medium of popular music, radio formatting became a science, and all lack-of-hell broke loose.

As the new century dawns, we are left with a polarized scene consisting of rouge (Shania Twain) and rage (Courtney Love), boyz ('N Sync) and noise (Korn). Every contemporary style, from gangsta rap to speed metal to new country to acid jazz, has been compartmentalized. Music fans establish their allegiances early, and never get the kind of cross-genre exposure that was commonplace in the first half of the seventies (see *Precious and Few: Pop Music in the Early '70s*). Popular music has splintered, probably permanently, into a million nondefinitive pieces.

Where are today's Sinatras, Elvises, Lennon and McCartneys? They are surfing the Internet, reading 'zines about their favorite act, dissing everything but their chosen substyle, losing the thread of popular-music history, adjusting their blinders. Like the cinema, music has become a blockbuster factory, trampling (or ignoring) the innovators that used to be its lifeblood. It seems grimly appropriate that, two decades after the groundwork for this sorry situation was laid, *Star Wars* is once again a going concern.

Should we blame the late seventies for all of this? God, yes. It will be fun.

Bar Wars

DISCO

"Get Up and Boogie (That's Right)" • Silver Convention (Midland I., 1976)
"Turn the Beat Around" • Vicki Sue Robinson (RCA, 1976)
"(Shake, Shake, Shake) Shake Your Booty" • K.C. and the Sunshine Band
(T.K., 1976)
"Love Hangover" • Diana Ross (Motown, 1976)
"Boogie Nights" • Heatwave (Epic, 1977)
"Last Dance" • Donna Summer (Casablanca, 1978)
"Y.M.C.A." • Village People (Casablanca, 1978)
"Le Freak" • Chic (Atlantic, 1978)
"Disco Inferno" • The Trammps (Atlantic, 1978)
"Don't Stop 'Til You Get Enough" • Michael Jackson (Epic, 1979)

"Yowsah, yowsah, yowsah." The phrase comes from *They Shoot Horses, Don't They?*—Sydney Pollack's film about the grim, grueling dance marathons of the thirties. When Chic used it on their 1977 debut single ("Dance, Dance, Dance [Yowsah, Yowsah, Yowsah]"), it suggested America had become one big, smoky, loud, interminable, joyless party. The idea was not without merit; a look inside any of the country's ten thousand discos presented a superficially celebratory but ultimately dispiriting picture. Surrounded by flashing lights, dry ice, and jackhammer-level sound, humanoids in genital-crushing designer jeans whirled and bobbed in predetermined patterns, blowing their tiny "disco whistles" at intervals as though officiating at some cybernetic sporting event. An endless stream of drum and bass information left room neither for conversation nor contemplation. Above the antiseptic din, a detached female voice chanted an ironic reprise: "I feel love, I feel love . . ." Disco, the century's most popular dance music, seemed the opposite of fun.

Or not—there are those who remember the disco era as a time of explosive release, peopled by free spirits sharing the communal joy of rhythm. Cocktails came with umbrellas, suits came with vests, and strangers came together.

Certainly disco had, in its formative days, produced some of the best pop singles of the mid-seventies—"Bad Luck," "Love's Theme," "Once You Get Started," "The Love I Lost," "T.S.O.P. (The Sound of Philadelphia)"—but most of those had come under the heading of "Philly soul," the highly orchestrated, rhythmically intoxicating style that by decade's end was disappearing faster than cocaine on a mirrored tabletop. (After 1976, only scattered gems like McFadden and Whitehead's "Ain't No Stoppin' Us Now" and the Jacksons' "Enjoy Yourself" hinted at the undiluted Nixon-era greatness of Philly gurus Kenny Gamble and Leon Huff.) Standard-issue disco was, by contrast, predictable.

From the emotionless drone of the Andrea True Connection's "More, More, More (Part 1)" to the intolerable pseudo-intensity of Patrick Hernandez's "Born to Be Alive," disco seemed irredeemably dull, attracting two detractors for every supporter. K.C. mercilessly exploited his "booty"/"boogie" formula. Boney M (brainchild of future Milli Vanilli creator Frank Farian) declawed Caribbean music. Meco added standard-issue thump to sci-fi movie themes. And, in what may well turn out to be pop culture's darkest hour, Gloria Gaynor's "I Will Survive" went to number one.

Of course, there were individual records that resisted or transcended disco's oppressive formalism. Michael Jackson's first Quincy Jones collaboration (1979's *Off the Wall*, including "Don't Stop 'Til You Get Enough" and the sparkling "Rock with You") was the very model of a modern major general-interest album. The Emotions, a former Stax/Volt trio whose artistic rebirth was overseen by Maurice White, cut "Best of My Love," disco's happiest hit. Diana Ross imbued "Love Hangover" with palpable morning-after lust and a killer fade (later appropriated by Gamble and Huff for Thelma Houston's "Don't Leave Me This Way"). The Trammps, fronted by Philly session vet Earl Young, spurred record smoke-detector sales in 1977 with "Disco Inferno," a four-alarm party record that was equal parts MFSB and EWF.

Part of the de-Philly-fication of disco was the music's return to its natural center, New York City. In addition to local acts like Chic, the Village People, GQ, Brass Construction, and Dr. Buzzard's Original "Savannah" Band, and tributes like "Native New Yorker" and "N.Y., You Got Me Dancing," New York was home to the swankiest, starfuckingest disco in the world, Steve Rubell's Studio 54. With its celebrity-studded guest list and impenetrable velvet rope, '54 represented the disco lifestyle at its excessive, elitist best. Infamous for its laissez-faire attitude toward nudity and drug use, it became the target for all who hated the D-word—a kind of boogie bogeyman. Not that the denizens of '54 were concerned; the upstanding citizens of Middle America lay outside the 212, and were, by definition, invisible.

Chic, disco's critical darlings and one of a handful of acts who mixed muscular, R&B-style playing with their hypnotic two- and three-chord vamps, were the kingpins of the New York sound. Guitarist Nile Rodgers and bassist Bernard Edwards crafted a string of hits not only for Chic ("Le Freak," "I Want Your Love," "Good Times"), but also Sister Sledge ("We Are Family," "He's the Greatest Dancer") and Diana Ross ("I'm Coming Out," "Upside Down").

THE FLOATING WORLD

Tonight, your wildest disco dreams come true.
In the Holiday Inn (Chestnut St.), just behind City Hall.
Disco starts at 7 p.m.

On the camp side, there were the Village People, a gay-themed act whose gold hits included the barely grooving "Y.M.C.A.," "Macho Man," and "In the Navy," and Dr. Buzzard's Original "Savannah" Band, a faux swing group that later evolved into Kid Creole and the Coconuts. Donna Summer, the Boston-born chanteuse who turned out to be disco's biggest star, lent her name to dance-floor fodder as uninspired as "Heaven Knows," and as beguiling as "Last Dance." (Note to seventies purists: Summer's best single, "On the Radio," came out in 1980.)

Both Summer and the Village People recorded for Casablanca Records, the New York label that, true to its name, was the White House of disco. Due south, outside Miami, T.K. Studios was home to another empire—that of K.C. and the Sunshine Band and related artists like Jimmy "Bo" Horne and George McCrae. Though McCrae's 1974 proto-disco hit "Rock Your Baby" was undoubtedly the most interesting record Harry Wayne Casey (K.C.) and partner Richard Finch ever produced, the duo exerted an almost Beatles-like hold on the pop and R&B charts from 1975 to 1977: "Get Down Tonight," "That's the Way (I Like It)," "(Shake, Shake, Shake) Shake Your Booty," and "I'm Your Boogie Man," while monozygotically alike, were popular in the extreme.

Disco was booming, especially in the U.S. The Recording Industry Association of America began certifying platinum (2 million–selling) singles in 1976, beginning with Johnnie Taylor's "Disco Lady" and continuing with "Boogie Nights," "Le Freak," "Bad Girls," "Stayin' Alive," "Boogie Oogie Oogie," and "Don't Stop 'Til You Get Enough." All-disco radio stations appeared and prospered. (". . . And now, for a change of pace, a little something at one hundred and twenty-*one* beats per minute!") Disco cinema's great trilogy—*Thank God It's Friday, Can't Stop the Music,* and *Saturday Night Fever*— brought the nightclub into the movie theater, with *Fever* and the Bee Gees de-ghettoizing the music, and *Friday* showing us the single most uncomfortable, herky-jerky performance of the era: decathlete-cum-actor Bruce Jenner getting down to the Village People. Rock stronghold *Rolling Stone* featured Donna Summer, the Village People, and the Bee Gees on its covers. In 1979, disco songs accounted for more than half of *Billboard*'s number one records.

Dan Rather called the whole phenomenon "another episode of silliness," and indeed discomania had some bizarre side effects: disco records by Cheryl Ladd, Ethel Merman, and Charo; roller disco, disco jazz, and disco reggae; wraparound skirts; power-mad doormen; Grace Jones. But, on the bright side, the genre brought public attention to the producer's role in pop music. Rodgers-Edwards, Casey-Finch, Quincy Jones, Maurice White, and techno-godfather Giorgio Moroder became, in some cases, as important as the artists they produced.

Moroder's groundbreaking work with Donna Summer in the field of breathing to the beat was not anomalous; in the era of *Looking for Mr. Goodbar,* sexual themes were plentiful. Propositions ("Kiss You All Over"), primers ("In the

Bush"), even warnings ("You Can't Turn Me Off [In the Middle of Turning Me On]") made the charts, and pre-AIDS (heck, pre-*herpes*) promiscuity was the order of the day. Bumping and hustling fell by the wayside as a new, crotch-grinding dance called "the freak" took hold. Album titles included *French Kiss, Bodyheat, Long Stroke, Nice 'n' Naasty,* and *Eargasm.*

Where could established stars go for a piece of this action? To the front of the line, of course. Steely Dan's acknowledged disco influence revealed itself engagingly on singles like "Peg" and "The Fez." The Rolling Stones had their biggest hit in five years with the disco-tinged "Miss You." Adult-contemporary icon Barbra Streisand teamed up with adult-content icon Donna Summer for the self-descriptive "No More Tears (Enough Is Enough)." James Brown hung up his "Godfather of Soul" title temporarily to become *The Original Disco Man.* Other disco dabblers included:

- Rod Stewart—"Da Ya Think I'm Sexy?"
- Elton John—"Bite Your Lip (Get Up and Dance!)"
- KISS—"I Was Made for Loving You"
- Isaac Hayes—"Juicy Fruit (Disco Freak) Pt. 1"
- Earth, Wind and Fire—"Boogie Wonderland"
- Cher—"Take Me Home"
- Dolly Parton—"Baby I'm Burnin'"
- Isley Brothers—"It's a Disco Night (Rock, Don't Stop)"
- Ohio Players—"Feel the Beat (Everybody Disco)"
- Boz Scaggs—"Hollywood"
- The Undisputed Truth—"Let's Go Down to the Disco"
- Queen—"Another One Bites the Dust."

Lest we conclude that disco was a strictly American phenomenon, it's worth noting that its practitioners also came from Germany (Silver Convention, Heatwave), the West Indies (Hot Chocolate, Boney M), France (Cerrone), Jamaica (Eruption), Cuba (Foxy), Italy (Giorgio Moroder), England (Gonzalez), Canada (Gino Soccio), and Japan (Pink Lady).

For rock fans, the music's country of origin was not the point—listening to disco from *anywhere* was comparable to having a tooth filled by Sir Laurence Olivier. Rockers from Joey Ramone to David Gilmour were unflinching in their condemnation. Frank Zappa, composer of "Disco Boy," wrote: "Disco entertainments centers make it possible for mellow, laid-back, boring kinds of people to meet each other and reproduce." The success of the chart-topping, grimly unfunny spoof "Disco Duck" was an indication of just how desperate the world was to have a laugh at disco's expense.

Unlike Paul Masson, which, according to then-pitchman Orson Welles, would "sell no wine before its time," record labels were signing anything with a beat and rushing it into the marketplace. When millions of hair dryers were recalled in 1979 because of harmful levels of asbestos, the blow-dried, hirsute music industry should have recognized it as some kind of omen: record sales would drop almost 20 percent by the end of the year. Despite the unbroken stream of low-maintenance best-sellers foretold by *Saturday Night Fever,* the crash had come, and major-label rosters were crowded with quick-buck, go-nowhere acts whose market value (and growth potential) was nil. As good as singles like Vicki Sue Robinson's "Turn the Beat Around," Evelyn "Champagne" King's "Shame," and Cheryl Lynn's "Got to Be Real" were, they were not the stuff of long-term careers; only a handful of disco types (Michael Jackson, Kool and the Gang, and a born-again Donna Summer) made it past the first few years of the 1980s.

The Japanese auto industry had embraced cybernetics, but

the American record industry had discovered it couldn't use robots to manufacture its product. Disco deservedly vaporized at decade's end, and the more danceable chart-toppers of 1980 and 1981 were fuelled by goofy synth effects ("Funkytown"), pseudo hip-hop ("Rapture"), proven hooks (Stars On 45's "Medley"), or unstoppable trends ("Physical"). The now jaded, recession-plagued pop audience that had willingly taken a ride in the stretch limo called disco would no longer be fooled by strangers in passing cars soliciting a quick buck.

Toot toot.

Hey!

Beep beep.

ROLL OVER, BEETHOVEN: Disco Discovers Covers

- "A Fifth of Beethoven"—Walter Murphy and the Big Apple Band
  (Ludwig van Beethoven, 1805–1807)
- "Whispering/Cherchez la femme/Se si bon"
  —Dr. Buzzard's Original "Savannah" Band
  (Paul Whiteman, 1920; Eartha Kitt, 1953)
- "If It's the Last Thing I Do"—Thelma Houston
  (Tommy Dorsey, 1937)
- "Chattanooga Choo-Choo"—Tuxedo Junction
  (Glenn Miller, 1941)
- "Tangerine"—Salsoul Orchestra
  (Jimmy Dorsey, 1942)
- "Brazil"—The Ritchie Family
  (Xavier Cugat, 1943)
- "Short Shorts"—Salsoul Orchestra
  (Royal Teens, 1958)
- "Dancing in the Street"—Boney M
  (Martha and the Vandellas, 1964)

- "Don't Let Me Be Misunderstood"—Santa Esmerelda
  (The Animals, 1965)
- "Knock On Wood"—Amii Stewart
  (Eddie Floyd, 1966)
- "MacArthur Park"—Donna Summer
  (Richard Harris, 1968)
- "I Can't Stand the Rain"—Eruption
  (Ann Peebles, 1973)
- "Uptown Festival (Part 1)"—Shalamar
  (medley of Motown hits)
- "Discomania (Part 1)"—Cafe Creme
  (medley of Beatles hits)

Take the Money and Run

POP

"Don't Go Breaking My Heart" • Elton John and Kiki Dee (Rocket, 1976)
"If You Leave Me Now" • Chicago (Columbia, 1976)
"Show Me the Way" • Peter Frampton (A&M, 1976)
"Silly Love Songs" • Wings (Capitol, 1976)
"Tonight's the Night (Gonna Be Alright)" • Rod Stewart (Warner Bros., 1976)
"Afternoon Delight" • Starland Vocal Band (Windsong, 1976)
"Moonlight Feels Right" • Starbuck (Private Stock, 1976)
"Rich Girl" • Daryl Hall & John Oates (RCA, 1977)
"Jet Airliner" • Steve Miller Band (Capitol, 1977)
"Dancing Queen" • ABBA (Atlantic, 1977)

When Howard Hughes died in 1976, the fortune hunters started coming out of the woodwork. Armed with forged versions of the late tycoon's last will and testament, the alleged former lovers and illegitimate children staked their claims (one woman, obviously underprepared, swore she was Hughes's manicurist). The unassuming Melvin Dumar, who swore to having given Hughes a ride in his truck, had a story compelling enough for Twentieth Century–Fox to get involved (*Melvin and Howard*, 1977).

Hughes's estate wasn't the only game in town: there was a lot of money up for grabs in the late seventies. With sixties idealism slipping into darkness, the entertainment industry became energized by mechanical sharks and high-powered talent agents (also mechanical sharks). Into this economic arena—sorry, *stadium*—stepped Peter Frampton, whose double album *Frampton Comes Alive!* became the first of several infamous late-seventies musical blockbusters. A true live album—you could hear the hall's echo, and the performances were overdub-free—*Alive!* featured Frampton's mellifluous, "talkbox"-enhanced guitar solos and winning pop songs like "Baby, I Love Your Way" and "Do You Feel Like We Do." Although Frampton would soon find his star descending, due largely to the sodden studio follow-up *I'm In You*, he had changed the economics of rock.

Rod Stewart, for one, took full advantage. Although he'd had other hits—"Maggie May," his ode to an older lover, had spent five weeks at number one in 1971—he was in the midst of a four-year dry spell when he followed Frampton's lead and came alive himself, with "Tonight's the Night (Gonna Be Alright)" in 1976. This time Stewart spent a whopping eight

weeks atop the charts, with the song reversing the (Maggie) May-December romance and walking a thin line between lechery and tenderness as the singer invited his "virgin child" to spread her "wings" and let him "come inside." It wasn't subtle, but it was lucrative. Rod's subsequent string of hits, though often verging on self-parody (well, come on, da *ya* think he's sexy?), was by turns solemn and campy ("The Killing of Georgie [Part I and II]," "Hot Legs").

The Steve Miller Band, and Daryl Hall and John Oates, two acts that had acquired substantial pre-1976 credibility with little help from AM radio, went into high gear in the late seventies. Miller, who had scored once before with "The Joker," kicked off a series of funky, if calculated, blues-pop hits with "Take the Money and Run," landing in the Top Ten three consecutive times with "Fly Like an Eagle," "Jet Airliner" and "Rock 'n Me." Philadelphia's Hall and Oates (file under "blue-eyed Philly soul") were weaned on the sounds of their city, and the results were obvious on "Sara Smile" (number 4, 1976) and "She's Gone" (number 7, 1976). The following year, scaling the charts with "Rich Girl," the two were well on their way to becoming history's most commercially successful vocal duo.

As a one-shot vocal duo, Elton John and Kiki Dee didn't do badly either, commercially speaking. "Don't Go Breaking My Heart," a strangely needy duet—why are they both so insecure?—damn near ruined the summer of '76 and became both the worst and most successful record of John's career (call it his "I Just Called to Say I Love You"). The song began a swift creative decline for the tunesmith; in 1979, when Philly soul mogul Thom Bell convinced Elton John he had a viable soul voice, pop lost one of its purest sounds.

Paul McCartney, another pop great in the midst of a late-seventies creative slide (compare 1975's *Venus and Mars* to

1976's *Wings at the Speed of Sound*), decided it was time somebody stuck up for "Silly Love Songs," so he wrote one. The result, a trite, number one trifle, became the most successful single of his career. McCartney, a full-time Wings commander throughout the late seventies, followed with more silly singles, the silliest being 1976's "Let 'Em In," a song about answering the door.

By contrast, still in their best years and sailing into the late seventies with a full head of creative steam, were Chicago. *Chicago X* (1976) was a typically mixed collection, but as always, the thrillers outweighed the filler. The album included the euphoric, Latin-tinged "Another Rainy Day in New York City." The followup, *Chicago XI* (1977), was the last to feature gruff-voiced lead guitarist Terry Kath, who died of an apparently accidental self-inflicted gunshot wound in early 1978. On these two records, vintage Chicago fare like "Little One," "Take Me Back to Chicago," and "You Are On My Mind" went more or less unnoticed partly because the band was peddling sugary Peter Cetera vehicles like "If You Leave Me Now" and "Baby, What a Big Surprise" (slow dancers, hit your marks). Things went south around the time the band temporarily ditched the roman-numeral album titles for 1978's *Hot Streets*.

Two softcore pop tunes from the summer of 1976 helped fight the "Don't Go Breaking My Heart" blues: Starland Vocal Band (SVB) and Starbuck (no relation) gave us "Afternoon Delight" and "Moonlight Feels Right," respectively. Signees to John Denver's Windsong label, SVB won the 1976 Best New Artist Grammy on the strength of "Afternoon Delight," a midday make-out anthem that sounded as all-American as Mark Spitz. "Moonlight Feels Right," an indelible jazz-pop romp punctuated by a lengthy marimba solo, found mellow singer Bruce Blackman laughing at his own sexual wordplay—"wet kiss . . . make the tide rise again"—and leaving a full eight beats between "moonlight" and "feels right."

These one-hit wonders, and other rare radio presences like Todd Rundgren ("Can We Still Be Friends"), Walter Egan ("Magnet and Steel"), Klaatu ("Sub-Rosa Subway"), Gerry Rafferty ("Baker Street"), Maxine Nightingale ("Right Back Where We Started From"), and Elvin Bishop ("Fooled Around and Fell In Love") hearkened back to singular early-seventies smashes like "Brandy," "Dancing in the Moonlight," and "Don't Pull Your Love," and to a time a little less money-obsessed than the Frampton era. (Big earners like Fleetwood Mac, Billy Joel, the Eagles, and the Bee Gees are covered separately in this book.)

A last vignette relevant to the fall-into-step, embrace-the-mainstream late seventies. One day in 1977, the residents of Steamwood, Illinois, a Chicago suburb, held a community parade. The new wrinkle was the parade's musical soundtrack—hundreds of transistor radios tuned to the same station. It's tempting to speculate on what platinum hits might have echoed through the streets of Steamwood in all their tinny glory that afternoon: could one of them have been ABBA's "Dancing Queen"—a sad, limp fistful of the international currency called Europop, and, just maybe, the scariest hit of the seventies? Might the locals have fallen into a Stepfordlike trance, marching in the middle of the road, eyes fixed on an imaginary, all-powerful pop center? And if all of this happened, why couldn't George Orwell have lived to see it?

Wild and Crazy Guys

NOVELTY RECORDS

"Disco Duck (Part 1)" • Rick Dees & His Cast of Idiots (RSO, 1976)
"Muskrat Love" • The Captain & Tennille (A&M, 1976)
"Short People" • Randy Newman (Warner Bros., 1977)
"Ain't Gonna Bump No More (With No Big Fat Woman)" • Joe Tex (Epic, 1977)
"Dreadlock Holiday" • 10cc (Mercury, 1978)
"King Tut" • Steve Martin with the Toot Uncommons (Warner Bros., 1978)
"Werewolves of London" • Warren Zevon (Asylum, 1978)
"Escape (The Piña Colada Song)" • Rupert Holmes (Infinity, 1979)
"Pop Muzik" • M (Sire, 1979)
"Video Killed the Radio Star" • The Buggles (Island, 1979)

When you think culture, you think Culture Club. You get misty about "early Whitney." You assume Richard and Linda Thompson are Twins. You consider Soft Cell musical pioneers. Bananarama?—underrated. Your first word was "Kajagoogoo-ga-ga." Your first sentence was, "Wake me up before you go-go-ga-ga." A-ha! You came of age in the eighties. Here is your comeuppance.

"Dee plane! Dee plane!"

Do you see him? It's Tattoo, played by Herve Villechaize. And look—there's Mr. Roarke, played by a marvelous-looking Ricardo Montalban; he's overseeing the arrival of a new crop of guests. You're among them, and as you deplane and descend the plane's stairs to the sunbaked tarmac, it hits you: this isn't a television show. It's your (glamorous) life.

You've been sent here to atone for your sins of omission. Like so many others who grew up with the seventies reflected in a Reagan-era rearview mirror ("CAUTION: OBJECTS WILL APPEAR SMALLER . . ."), you have reduced an entire decade, whose pop riches include peak Joni, peak Bowie, peak Stevie, and peak Steely, into one bad junior-high house party. Shame on you. You will pay for your careless oversimplification by doing time in a world forsaken by God, a world of dancing waterfowl, rutting rodents, and Carnaby Street carnivores. It's a world that very nearly lives up to your narrow view of the seventies. Welcome, my hair gel–slopping, megamall-shopping friend, to Novelty Island.

Tattoo hustles you into a dimly lit, shag-carpeted basement—a "rec room," in seventies parlance—and locks the door from the outside. The only furniture is a plaid La-Z-Boy recliner. It's situated beside a Radio Shack sound system, a "Realistic," complete with penny-weighted tone arm. Next to the stereo, there's a stack of scratchy singles (what your older siblings call "forty-fives"). The only sound is the slow, agonizing *drip-drip-drip* of an unseen tap. You sit in the chair and wait. An hour passes.

Drip.

Drip.

Drip.

Finally, you turn to the stereo in desperation, hoping to obscure the sound of the water. To your dismay, the singles are labeled simply "Late Seventies Novelties." You grab the top one and reluctantly slide it over the turntable's yellow plastic 45-RPM adapter. The needle hits the record, and "Disco Duck (Part 1)" floods the room. With a self-satisfied grin, you lean back in your chair. You've been given a few moments to feel superior—listening to Rick Dees and His Cast of Idiots does that for people.

"Disco Duck" was a tip of the hat to Jackie Lee's 1965 dance record "The Duck," and it took Dees, a Memphis "morning man" on WMPS-AM, to the top of the charts in 1976. After losing his job when he mentioned the song on the air—conflict of interest!—Dees got a new gig at neighboring WHBQ-AM and continued to release records ("Dis-Gorilla," "Get Nekked," and "Eat My Shorts," to name a few), none of which made the Top 40.

But you're not interested in Dees's curriculum vitae. You're busy tarring an entire decade with his brush, listening smugly to his lame Donald Duck impression. As the song's rote dance beat reconfirms everything you've always thought about the seventies, you chuckle, "'Part One'? You mean there's a 'Disco Duck (Part *Two*)'?" Ha-ha. Ha. Heh. You begin to feel better about Toni Basil.

The song ends. Compared to Rick Dees, the dripping tap

isn't so annoying. It starts to grate again after a couple of minutes, though, and you decide to work through the rest of the pile. Next up: the nonsensical Europop smash "Pop Muzik." What a goofy song, you think, as your toe involuntarily keeps time. Recorded by Robin Scott (who took his professional moniker from the "M" on Paris's Metro signs), "Pop Muzik" was interesting in 1979 because it not only had nothing to say, it was *about* having nothing to say. But you're a child of the eighties—you came of age surrounded by postmodern, self-referential music—and this seems not at all remarkable.

Record number three is "Muskrat Love" by the Captain (former Beach Boys sideman Daryl Dragon) and Tennille (Dragon's wife and lead singer Toni—no relation to Tony! Toni! Toné!). The pair, who began a string of Javex-white hits in 1975 with "Love Will Keep Us Together," got musky in 1976 with the story of two frisky aquatic rodents named Susie and Sam ("muzzle to muzzle . . . they wiggle"), and wound up at number 4. A year earlier, America, a trio famous for a song about an animal "with no name," had scored a minor hit with the original version of the song, about two animals *with* names. However, apart from sounding like a good handle for a quirky adult Web site (click on my water-repellent fur for red-hot action!), "Muskrat Love" barely holds your interest.

Suddenly, you snap to attention as Joe Tex's "Ain't Gonna Bump No More (with No Big Fat Woman)" fills the room with its earthy, girthy funk. "She did a dip," Tex grunts. "Almost broke my hip." Although you laud the singer's decision to forsake "the bump"—a stupid seventies ritual by all accounts, and not nearly as cool as that dance-without-moving-your-feet, cheeks-sucked-in Duran Duran step you remember from junior high—you can't abide his politically incorrect attitude toward women. (Tex, possibly the first R&B singer to be known as a "rapper" [*From the Roots Came the Rapper*], was never p.c.; check out his 1972 hit "I Gotcha" for even dicier lyrics.)

More forty-fives follow: "The Fonz Song" by the Heyettes; "Up Your Nose with a Rubber Hose" by Gabe Kaplan; "Junk Food Junkie" by Larry Groce; "Bloat On" by Cheech and Chong; "Kong" by Dickie Goodman; "Turn Loose of My Leg" by Jim Stafford; "I Need Your Help, Barry Manilow" by Ray Stevens; "Do You Think I'm Disco" by Steve Dahl . . . Ian Dury's Monty-Python-on-steroids hits "Sex & Drugs & Rock & Roll" and "Hit Me With Your Rhythm Stick" enliven the proceedings. Rupert Holmes's "Escape"—not incidentally, the last number one song of the seventies—comes on, and you find yourself singing along with the "if you like piña coladas" part. Shaken, you remove the record. The *drip, drip, drip* returns, but it serves only to remind you of the next lyric: "gettin' caught in the rain."

This pile of hits has reinforced every narrow idea you've ever had about the seventies, and now you want out. But the room—locked, windowless, decorated in early sitcom—discourages any thought of escape (or, indeed, piña coladas), so you decide to sift through the rest of the records, novelties all.

The next few are, you allow, more interesting; not just stupid and offensive, but *knowingly* stupid and offensive, relics of ironic pop's first bloom. Here, for example, is Steve Martin's "King Tut," a hilariously irreverent commentary on Tutmania, the late-seventies hypefest that accompanied the North American museum tour of Tutankhamen's remains. Here, too, is an intentionally soulless version of "(I Can't Get No) Satisfaction" by Devo—short for "de-evolution"—complete with clipped, robotic vocals and upside-down-flowerpot hats. And here is "Werewolves of London," Warren Zevon's lycanthropic signature tune . . . perhaps, you think, an inspiration for the 1981 film *American Werewolf In London.*

You realize you're actually enjoying yourself as you get to the second-to-last record in the pile. It's Randy Newman's "Short People" (from 1977's *Little Criminals*), and for the first time you grasp the song's biting send-up of prejudice. Newman—whose rich catalog too often has been marginalized—has confessed to mixed feelings about the song's success (he once compared it to "Purple People Eater"), but "Short People"'s caustic first-person satire is vintage Newman. Like "Sail Away" and "Rednecks," it— it—

All at once, you're awake. You were dreaming. You're home in bed, and your digital clock radio, which has been on for some time, is playing the closing seconds of the Buggles' prescient eve-of-the-eighties hit, "Video Killed the Radio Star." Another ironic late-seventies novelty hit, "Video" was, appropriately, the first clip to be aired on the fledgling MTV network in 1981.

The song ends, and from the radio comes the voice of a Deeslike morning man: "Hey, early risers, that concludes another 'Seventies-at-Seven Super Session!' This morning we featured some novelty tunes sent to us by two listeners who need to get out more. Thanks, guys. We'll take the seventh caller now, for that solid gold Kama Sutra coffeepot . . ."

You make a mental note to fix the leaky tap in the bathroom down the hall (and to get out more). Then you sit up in bed, silently thank God for binary code, and plop the closest compact disc into your Discman. The clinical thump of your favorite decade returns. It's The Human League. You remember the good old days, when Paul Young and Mick Hucknall could pass for soul singers, when the perfect woman had "Bette Davis Eyes" and not only "Legs," but a working knowledge of them. Drunk on cheap nostalgia, you call the radio station and request "99 Luftballoons." The dream fades. You've learned nothing.

Photo credit: Jeff Burke

Don with Monty Python's Eric Idle at a book signing in 1976.

Last Tango

EARLY SEVENTIES, CONTINUED

"Keep Me Cryin' " • Al Green (Hi, 1976)
"Cupid" • Tony Orlando & Dawn (Elektra, 1976)
"Summer" • War (United Artists, 1976)
"Get Closer" • Seals & Crofts (Warner Bros., 1976)
"Stand Tall" • Burton Cummings (Portrait, 1976)
"My Sweet Lady" • John Denver (RCA, 1977)
"Hard Rock Cafe" • Carole King (Capitol, 1977)
"(Remember the Days of the) Old Schoolyard" • Cat Stevens (A&M, 1977)
"It's Ecstasy When You Lay Down Next to Me" • Barry White (20th Century, 1977)
"Don't Worry Baby" • B.J. Thomas (MCA, 1977)

"I've got a feeling we'll be seeing each other again," sang Al Wilson in 1976. Turns out he was wrong. Wilson, the Mississippi-born soul crooner known for 1973's "Show and Tell," would never again revisit the *Billboard* Hot 100. And he was just one of a surprising number of major early-seventies "singles acts" who effectively disappeared from view after 1975.

In several high-profile instances, the commercial swan dives seemed to have been decreed from above. Among the artists experiencing new religious fervor in the late seventies, Memphis soul veteran Al Green was undoubtedly the best known. After dominating the Top 40 during the early seventies, the newly ordained Reverend Green revisited his old neighborhood one more time in 1976 with the Willie

Mitchell–produced "Keep Me Cryin'." He would thereafter become more and more conflicted about his affinity for both sacred and secular subject matter. It was a dichotomy that had haunted him since his teens, when his father had barred him from performing with his siblings in the Greene Brothers for listening to the "profane" R&B music of Jackie Wilson. By 1979, Green had put his pop career on hold indefinitely, having understood an accident in Cincinnati (he fell off a stage) to be a warning from God. He released *The Lord Will Make a Way* the next year. The seventies were over, and so was the Reverend's "Sha-La-La" period.

Another artist who switched from pop to gospel, a move that virtually guaranteed a hit-free future, was middle-of-the-road (MOR) stalwart B.J. Thomas. Between 1966 and 1975, he had enjoyed a run of thirteen Top 40 singles, including the prescient "Mighty Clouds of Joy." In 1976, after a chart-topping wallow called "(Hey Won't You Play) Another Somebody Done Somebody Wrong Song," the artist formerly known as Billy Joe turned his attention to gospel songs, finding the Top 40 only once more (with a cover of Brian Wilson's "Don't Worry Baby").

For Tony Orlando, the man who made yellow ribbons America's favorite homecoming symbol, the fateful religious epiphany came in 1977. His television show had been canceled, and his final Top 40 hit, a 1976 cover of Sam Cooke's "Cupid," had come and gone. So, too, had his close friend Freddie *(Chico and the Man)* Prinze, whose much-publicized suicide had hit the singer hard. In July 1977, Orlando announced to a packed house in Cohasset, Massachusetts, that Jesus Christ had knocked three times on his ceiling (okay, we're paraphrasing), and that he would be retiring that very night.

Cat "Peace Train" Stevens converted to the Muslim faith in

1979 at age thirty-two, taking the name Yusuf Islam. "(Remember the Days of the) Old Schoolyard" (number 33, 1977) was at the time his most recent hit—his hot streak for A&M was well and truly over—and American radio went on without him. (Stevens/Islam would command public attention again in 1989 when he announced his support of the *fatwa* [death sentence] placed on author Salman Rushdie by Muslim fundmentalists, for Rushdie's novel *The Satanic Verses.*)

John Denver saw God in the late seventies, too, and He looked like George Burns. Denver starred with Burns in the 1977 movie *Oh, God!*—a serviceable comedy in which a grocery-store manager encounters the droll, cigar-chomping Almighty, but it wasn't a religious insight that slowed the Country Boy's pace late in the decade: it was his dated agenda. Songs about sunshine, country roads, and the Rocky Mountains were seldom playlisted in an era that found so many music lovers indoors, in the dark, on the dance floor. Denver's average chart position in 1976 and 1977 was number 46, compared to a number 5 average the previous two years. Like so many other *Billboard* mainstays, he couldn't quite get over the mid-decade hump.

Dim, indoor lighting suited love god Barry White just fine. His lushly orchestrated disco come-ons were likely responsible for at least as many unplanned pregnancies as the 1977 New York City blackout, and he shared none of Al Green's inner conflict regarding the sacred and the profane (as White preached the gospel of "luuuv" from his specially reinforced soapbox, it seemed the profane *was* sacred). From 1973 to 1975, White had scored seven hits, not counting his productions for Love Unlimited and the Love Unlimited Orchestra. Unfortunately, like Denver, his late-seventies résumé contained only one hit, the near-rhyme, "It's Ecstasy When You Lay Down Next to Me."

Other formerly red-hot acts who found their careers in a post-'76 deep freeze included:

- War, whose "Summer" was grade-A beach music;
- Carole King, whose "Hard Rock Cafe" foreshadowed the soon-to-be-ubiquitous restaurant chain;
- Burton Cummings, whose "Stand Tall" was the former Guess Who leader's only Top Ten solo hit;
- Neil Sedaka, whose "Steppin' Out" featured Elton John on backup vocals;
- Three Dog Night, whose low-charting *American Pastime* indicated their time had indeed passed;
- Helen Reddy, whose "Make Love to Me" found few takers;
- Bread, whose "Lost Without Your Love" gave the wholesome balladeers one last bun in the oven;
- Rare Earth, whose "Warm Ride" was just that; and
- Lobo, whose "Where Were You When I Was Falling In Love" had millions answering, "Someplace else."

In some cases, the sputtering careers of these hitmakers could be blamed on creative exhaustion: Johnny Bristol, the man behind 1974's musical multiple orgasm "Hang On In There, Baby," had surely run out of ideas by the time he used his name for a cheap laugh on 1976's *Bristol's Creme*. For others, the book of love was tossed aside in favor of the Good Book. And sometimes, an artist's time was just plain *up*. With each disappearance, the pop landscape shifted a little. In Helen Reddy's case, very little.

Mr. Bill

BILLY JOEL

"Say Goodbye to Hollywood" • Ronnie Spector (Columbia, 1976)
"New York State of Mind" • Billy Joel (Columbia, 1976)
"Just the Way You Are" • Billy Joel (Columbia, 1977)
"Scenes from an Italian Restaurant" • Billy Joel (Columbia, 1977)
"Movin' Out (Anthony's Song)" • Billy Joel (Columbia, 1978)
"Only the Good Die Young" • Billy Joel (Columbia, 1978)
"She's Always a Woman" • Billy Joel (Columbia, 1978)
"My Life" • Billy Joel (Columbia, 1978)
"Big Shot" • Billy Joel (Columbia, 1979)
"Honesty" • Billy Joel (Columbia, 1979)

It's Saturday night, Anywhere, U.S.A., 1975. Elton John, keyboard-thumping troubadour du jour, is live at the Anywhere Arena. His stage attire—a gold lamé suit with feather boa and ten-story-high elevator shoes—is easily discernible even from the nosebleed section. Before the rapt crowd, the man they call Captain Fantastic pounds the insides out of his white grand piano, sings about a gang of beer-swilling toughs, and anthemically belabors the obvious: "Saturday! Saturday! Saturday night's all right!"

Three years later, same arena. Billy Joel, a former boxer, has inherited Elton John's crown. Less flamboyant than John—he is wearing a tweed jacket, white shirt, and jeans—but equally beloved, Joel mounts his black grand piano and makes like Jerry Lee Lewis. With a joyous sneer, he sings the mock praises of a pretentious "Big Shot," directly descended from Elton's Saturday-night warriors: "You sure did put on a show!"

John and Joel, consummate showmen both, were piano pop's one-two punch during the seventies. But despite Hall of Fame numbers and still-loyal followings, they reached their creative zeniths relatively early. In fact, long careers aside, E.J. and B.J. were at their best for only about five years each, their respective peaks bisecting the "Me Decade" right down the middle. Elton got the first half, and Billy, who was still a Los Angeles lounge lizard the year Elton scored his first number one record ("Crocodile Rock," 1973), got the second half.

The late seventies saw Billy Joel moving beyond the Harry Chapinesque songcraft of his early work, into "capital *P*" Pop, with a trilogy of New York–themed albums: *Turnstiles* (1976), *The Stranger* (1977), and *52nd Street* (1978). For a while, he was a kind of Top 40 Woody Allen, lovingly documenting the Big Apple in all its tumultuous glory. Like Allen, Joel used the city as his main "location," setting his stories on specific streets (42nd, 52nd, Broadway, Park Avenue, Riverside Drive), and incorporating local landmarks (the Empire State Building, Elaine's, Herald Square) and locales (Brooklyn, Harlem, Chinatown) into his lyrics. If Allen's muse was a $300-an-hour shrink in an office overlooking Central Park, Joel's was a welterweight chump in a gym overlooking Angelo's Restaurant. Both men "love[d] New York," to quote the then ubiquitous tourism jingle, but the feisty singer-songwriter's work was a little more streetwise.

Billy Joel's music didn't always have a 212 area code. During the early seventies, the Long Island native and his then wife and manager, Elizabeth, lived in California, and *Piano Man* (1973) and *Streetlife Serenade* (1974) reflected their Left Coast displacement: "Los Angelenos all come from somewhere," Joel crooned. Peppered with stops in Nevada, reveries in Paris, and Mexican connections, his songs were a far cry from the colorful Manhattan vignettes to come.

In January 1975, Joel moved back East. Within twenty minutes of his arrival, he had reportedly finished writing "New York State of Mind," a rhapsodic jazz ballad descended from "Autumn in New York" and "We'll Take Manhattan." Eventually appearing on *Turnstiles,* the song became a legitimate standard, due in part to a 1977 cover by Brooklyn's own Barbra Streisand (from the diva's *Superman* album).

If "New York State of Mind" was a meditation on Joel's escape to Gotham, "Say Goodbye to Hollywood," another *Turnstiles* track, was the parting glance in his rearview mirror. Intended as a tribute to Phil Spector, the song, like the album, was brilliant but woefully underproduced, and Joel's "wall of sound" was pure plywood. Fittingly, it was Spector's ex-wife Ronnie, namesake of the Ronettes, who first covered "Say Goodbye to Hollywood": Joel's own "cover" (from the live *Songs in the Attic*) went to number 17 in 1981. "Until the Night," a later Spector homage, proved more successful, thanks in part to the production savvy of another famous Phil—Ramone. Arguably the centerpiece of the Grammy-winning, Ramone-produced *52nd Street,* itself arguably the centerpiece of Joel's career, "Until the Night" would have made a righteous Righteous Brothers duet. Though never released as a single, it's the emotional backbone of Joel's catalog, a perfect fusion of the artist's ballsy spirit and retro-romanticism.

Given Joel's dual sensibilities—hey, this guy actually *was* a lover and a fighter—there was no better setting for his songs than New York City. At once tender and surly, sophisticated and vulgar, lively and lonely, the city would just as soon fatten your lip as kiss you good-night. Joel's iron fist was hidden in a velvet (boxing) glove, and the pug-with-a-heart-of-gold image was central to his appeal. He could deliver a sweet ballad like "Just the Way You Are" (the breakout track from *The Stranger*), then turn up the testosterone for a fast shuffle like "Only the Good Die Young," in effect whispering, "Don't go changing" in one ear and, "Please consider changing your religious faith so that we can have sexual intercourse," in the other. (What was a girl to think?)

Both songs were hits. Sure, "Just the Way You Are" has worn wafer-thin through more than two hundred cover versions (including Barry White's), but you can't blame that on the original, any more than you can hold Paul Simon responsible for the disco version of "Bridge Over Troubled Water." Joel's version was a shimmering mix of indelible melody, phase-shifted Fender Rhodes, acoustic guitar, and sinewy alto sax courtesy of jazz great Phil Woods. "Only the Good Die Young," banned by some stations for its perceived anti-Catholic bent (it was really just anticelibate), found Joel singing "Virginia, don't let me wait" with the lusty bravado of a sixteen-year-old.

Occasionally, both sides of the artist's persona could be heard on the same track. On the chorus of "Honesty," Joel out-Hallmarked Hallmark; then, on the bridge, out-Brandoed Brando. "She's Always a Woman," an arch ballad if ever there was one, could have lapsed into saccharine overload, had the seemingly benign title not been undercut by lines like "she'll carelessly cut you and laugh while you're bleeding."

"Stiletto" (1978), an R&B/S&M rave-up that once again featured a woman eager to "cut you," found Joel singing in the Ray Charles–style growl he'd previously used on "Weekend Song" and "Everybody Has a Dream." Unfortunately, it was a sound that would finally submerge his fresh, earnest tenor. At his best, Billy Joel sounded like an Italian-American Paul McCartney; he could vocally navigate even rangy, ambitious material like *The Stranger*'s "Scenes from an Italian Restaurant" suite (aka "Bottle o' Red").

Then, as now, the rock establishment undervalued Joel. Robert Christgau called him "the Irving Berlin of narcissistic alienation" and "a better Elton John than Leo Sayer," typifying the Billy-as-lightweight party line. But Joel, who used to exhort his audiences not to "take any shit from anybody," actually had plenty of angry young man in him, a fact that would dawn on *Rolling Stone*—too late—in 1980. The September *Stone* cover featured a portrait of the artist as a bug-eyed pugilist, and was emblazoned with the headline BILLY JOEL IS ANGRY; Mr. Sensitive, it seemed, was ready to rumble, and skeptics were being urged to look deeper. Alas, unless "It's Still Rock and Roll to Me" was your cup of tea, the call was two years too late.

Since his New York period, Joel has all too frequently squandered his gifts. With notable exceptions like "Allentown" (1982) and "An Innocent Man" (1983), he has vanished into a late-Elton, marginally melodic fog. That his stock has sagged as a result does not appear to have dimmed his spirit; he's still stubbornly self-determining, still electrifying live, and, yes, still the only singer ever to have played Yankee Stadium.

Sweathog Nation

BUBBLEGUM

"Money Honey" • Bay City Rollers (Arista, 1976)
"Boogie Fever" • The Sylvers (Capitol, 1976)
"Let Her In" • John Travolta (Midland I., 1976)
"Enjoy Yourself" • The Jacksons (Epic, 1976)
"C'mon Marianne" • Donny Osmond (Polydor, 1976)
"Ain't Nothing Like the Real Thing" • Donny & Marie Osmond (Polydor, 1976)
"Da Doo Ron Ron" • Shaun Cassidy (Warner Bros., 1977)
"Runaround Sue" • Leif Garrett (Atlantic, 1977)
"You're the One That I Want" • John Travolta and Olivia Newton-John (RSO, 1978)
"You Take My Breath Away" • Rex Smith (Columbia, 1979)

What's bubblegum? Think of it this way. You're navigating a crowded intersection on foot, your eyes fixed on the DON'T WALK sign you're disobeying, when suddenly you feel a slight tug on your left heel. Damn. There, on the sole of your shoe, is a freshly spat, glutinous pink wad. You pick at the offending substance with a stick. No good. You scrape your shoe on the curb. Still no good. The thing has made a home in the crevices of your sneakers, and it will live there until, one day (if you're lucky), it hardens and falls away unnoticed.

Now think of it another way. It's 1977. Jaywalking through a crowded intersection, narrowly avoiding Gremlins and Pacers, you stop dead in your tracks. Damn. You've just heard Shaun Cassidy's cloying cover of the Crystals' "Da Doo Ron Ron" drifting from a car window. It's not that you like the song—you really, really don't—but it sticks, and you now attempt to remove it by singing other, better songs: "Do / you / feel like I doo ron ron ron, da doo . . ." Face it. The thing has made a home in the crevices of your brain, and it will live there until, one day (if you're lucky) . . . et cetera, et cetera.

Bubblegum is gooey and sweet, and sticks even when you don't want it to. The first real bubblegum hits, highly adhesive confections like "Chewy Chewy" and "Goody Goody Gumdrops," were produced at Buddah Records in the late 1960s. In the early seventies, the torch was carried by real and fictitious musical families with surnames like Osmond, Jackson, Hudson, DeFranco, Brady, and Partridge.

By the late seventies, family pop was disappearing faster than licensed Erik Estrada merchandise. Its last shining moment came courtesy of the Sylvers, ten brothers and sisters from Memphis whose screechy chart-topper "Boogie Fever" was partially set in a pizza parlor. Despite teen-themed follow-ups like "Hot Line," "Cotton Candy," and "High School Dance," however, the Sylvers couldn't do it alone, and before long, the bubblegum family had begun to burst. Slowly, Mom-and-Pop popsters gave way to tanned, TV-tutored and/or tall, tartan-trimmed hunks.

No question: It was five blokes from Edinburgh, Scotland, who defined late-seventies bubblegum. But it was neither the Bay City Rollers' Florence Henderson haircuts nor their Brit-lite music that made the biggest impact; it was their tartan togs, a shout-it-from-the-heathered-hilltops fashion statement meant to identify the group as proudly Scottish. (Screaming Rollers fans were seen sporting tartan scarves, socks, knickers, kilts, tams, and face paint.) Christened in 1970 when their manager stuck a pin at random into a spinning globe and landed on Bay City, Michigan (whose unsuspecting residents inherited a crippling burden of guilt), the Rollers were already stars in the U.K. by mid-decade. But only in the U.K. Then broadcaster Howard Cosell "pulled a Sullivan," inviting the so-called "Prefab Five" onto his ABC variety show *Saturday Night* in September 1975, and Stateside Rollermania got under way. The Bay City Rollers sang "Saturday Night" on *Saturday Night* that Saturday night, and although it was more of a pep-rally chant than a song, it eventually went to number one in the U.S., sparking a two-year chart run for the plaid-clad lads.

Trumpeting bubblegum's return to the solo hunk—roll over Davy Jones, tell Bobby Sherman the news—were four actors:

- Rex Smith, a Broadway musical-theater star;
- Leif Garrett, who had appeared in the three *Walking Tall* films;
- John Travolta, who played well-meaning Vinnie Barbarino on *Welcome Back, Kotter;* and
- Shaun "My Name's Not Keith and That's Not a Partridge" Cassidy, one of television's *Hardy Boys.*

Travolta had but one solo hit—a pallid ballad called "Let Her In" (1976)—but enjoyed a little *Grease* overflow when "You're the One That I Want" and "Summer Nights," both duets with Olivia Newton-John, went Top Five in 1978. "Sexy Rexy" Smith struck gold with 1979's "You Take My Breath Away" (pronounced *"yteekmbreathaweee"*), and both Garrett and Cassidy released covers of old rock-and-roll tunes: the former, "Surfin' U.S.A.," "Runaround Sue," and "The Wanderer"; the latter, "Da Doo Ron Ron" and "Do You Believe in Magic." (The plunder-the-sixties approach was a proven formula for teen stars like Donny Osmond ["Puppy Love"] and Michael Jackson ["Rockin' Robin"].) Garrett's biggest success came in 1978 with the debatable "I Was Made for Dancin'."

Bubblegum's royal families, the Osmonds and Jacksons, stayed busy during the late seventies, but their dominance faded. Donny Osmond had a minor hit with the 4 Seasons' "C'mon Marianne," but the Osmond clan maintained their pop-cultural profile largely through television. *The Donny and Marie Hour* opened with the "little bit rock-and-roll" brother and the "little bit country" sister sparring verbally à la Sonny and Cher (without the sexual subtext), and lasted four years, prompting the release of two of the most sensibly titled albums of all time: *Donny and Marie—Featuring Songs from Their Television Show* and *Donny and Marie—New*

Season. Of the Donny and Marie movie, *Goin' Coconuts,* and Donny's solo album, *Discotrain*—the less said, the better.

The renamed "Jacksons" (sans Jermaine) left Motown for Epic in 1975, a move that inspired a $20 million breach-of-contract suit from Motown boss Berry Gordy Jr. (Jermaine's father-in-law). "Enjoy Yourself" and "Shake Your Body (Down to the Ground)" went platinum and enlivened dance floors, but the Jacksons' hits were now separated by years, not months. While CBS aired the requisite variety series (featuring all nine Jackson siblings, even little Janet), Michael laid the groundwork for his eventual world dominance: Starring in *The Wiz* in 1978, he befriended Quincy Jones, who would go on to produce *Off the Wall, Thriller,* and *Bad* (combined U.S. sales to date: 40 million).

Of course, neither the Osmonds nor the Jacksons would ever fully let go of the pop-family formula. In 1990, four of Alan Osmond's eight children would debut as the Osmond Boys and recycle Uncle Donny's 1971 hit "Hey Girl," itself a recycled version of Bobby Vee's 1968 hit, itself a recycled version of Freddie Scott's 1963 hit. In 1996, Tito Jackson's three sons would sign with Uncle Michael's MJJ label as "3T," because *they were all named Tito.*

Records by *Happy Days* co-stars Donny Most and Anson Williams . . .

Oh, never mind. The point is, during the late seventies, with divorce rates climbing, contraceptives being distributed to minors, and promiscuous singles setting the pop-culture agenda, family ties did not guarantee bubblegum success. A fresh crop of male "artists" took up the slack, allowing their erotomaniacal female fans to rehearse for the day when they would feel intense sexual longing for someone they'd actually met.

The legacy? Well, there are those among us who still have twenty-year-old bubblegum stuck in our shoes, and you may be one of us. Try the following test to find out.

1) When we say, "S-A-T-U-R-D-A-Y," you say: "_____!"
2) Is Boogie Fever contagious?
3) According to the 1978 single, what will the chicks do for "Greased Lightnin'"?
4) What was the full name of the Hudson Brothers' Saturday-morning show?
5) Leif "Runaround Sue" Garrett later sang about what similar character?
6) According to the Jacksons, you should blame all indiscretions on _____.
7) Name two oddball characters from John Travolta's career whose names rhyme.

ANSWERS: 1) "Night!" 2) Yes; "It's going around." 3) "The chicks'll cream." 4) *The Hudson Brothers Razzle Dazzle Comedy Show.* 5) "Runaway Rita." 6) "The boogie." 7) Barbarino/Tarantino.

Boogiespeak

BUZZWORDS

"Looking Out for #1" • Bachman-Turner Overdrive (Mercury, 1976)
"Laid Back Love" • Major Harris (Atlantic, 1976)
"Breaker-Breaker" • Outlaws (Arista, 1976)
"You Are My Starship" • Norman Connors (Buddah, 1976)
"Life in the Fast Lane" • The Eagles (Asylum, 1977)
"So Into You" • Atlanta Rhythm Section (Polydor, 1977)
"Do You Wanna Make Love" • Peter McCann (20th Century, 1977)
"Easy" • Commodores (Motown, 1977)
"Swayin' to the Music (Slow Dancin')" • Johnny Rivers (Big Tree, 1977)
"Boogie Shoes" • K.C. and the Sunshine Band (T.K., 1978)

"Looking Out for #1" wasn't just the dominant personal philosophy of the late seventies; it was also a best-selling book by Robert Ringer and a strangely jazzy 1976 single by Canadian blue-collar rockers Bachman-Turner Overdrive. At its simplest level, that's how pop culture works: a fresh idea, a new wrinkle in the zeitgeist (or, best of all, an actual catchphrase) filters down to the level of commercial artists and young consumers—and magic and/or money is made.

The Eagles' funky, cynical mini-masterpiece "Life in the Fast Lane" is a great example, although in that case the catchphrase didn't filter down from anywhere—Don Henley coined it himself. A grimly detailed document of the doped-up, alienated state of relationships in the age of the biorhythm, "Fast Lane" aimed far higher than opportunistic catchphrase singles like Bro Smith's "Bigfoot" (1976) and Rick Dees's "Bigfoot" (1978).

Bigfoot, who may in fact have been simply a lost hiker with a bitchin' 'fro, was a hot topic at the time. Equally hot was the CB radio craze, notable not only for trucker flicks like *Convoy* and *Breaker! Breaker!,* but for novelty pop songs like "Convoy" and "Breaker-Breaker." At the height of the fad, North America's airwaves were so thick with CB activity that commercial radio signals were being crowded out. (This may have been a good thing, since many of those signals were carrying songs like "Money Honey" and "I've Never Been to Me.")

Other musical trends included the *Star Wars*–induced science-fiction boom ("You Are My Starship," "Star Cruiser," "Spaceship Superstar"), vertical groping ("Swayin' to the Music [Slow Dancin']," "Slow Dancing," "Slow Dancin' Don't Turn Me On," "[Feel So Good] Slow Dancing"), and Sweathog slang ("Up Your Nose with a Rubber Hose"). Reggae's burgeoning popularity sparked the 10cc when-in-Rome saga "Dreadlock Holiday" (from the nouveaux-Beatles' underappreciated 1978 LP *Bloody Tourists*), and technology-inspired records as varied as "Instant Replay," "Funk-O-Nots," and "I'm Cathy's Clone."

Surely the biggest development in late-seventies catchphrase pop, though, was the abandonment of hippiespeak for boogiespeak. As recently as 1973, groovy slogans like "Hang Loose," "Do Your Thing," "What It Is," and "Keep On Truckin'" had been the basis of hit songs. But now Flower Power was as useless as a ream of Spiro Agnew's vice presidential letterhead. The easygoing, pot-induced goodwill of the early seventies had been replaced by horny, urban abandon, and pop's new lexicon was coming from the sexually charged atmosphere of the disco. To whit:

- **"Boogie"**

  "Boogie Child"—Bee Gees (1977)

  "Boogie Fever"—Sylvers (1976)

  "Boogie Nights"—Heatwave (1977)

  "Boogie Shoes"—K.C. and the Sunshine Band (1978)

  "Boogie Wonderland"—Earth, Wind and Fire (1979)

  "Boogie Oogie Oogie"—A Taste of Honey (1978)

  "Boogie Woogie Dancin' Shoes"—Claudja Barry (1979)

  "I'm Your Boogie Man"—K.C. and the Sunshine Band (1977)

- **"Do It"**

  "Can't Stop Groovin' Now, Wanna Do It Some More"—B.T. Express (1976)

  "Do It Good"—Taste of Honey (1979)

  "Do It or Die"—Atlanta Rhythm Section (1979)

  "Do It To My Mind"—Johnny Bristol (1977)

  "Do It with Feeling"—Michael Zager's Moon Band/Peabo Bryson (1976)

  "Doin' It"—Herbie Hancock (1976)

  "The More You Do It (The More I Like It Done to Me)"—Ronnie Dyson (1976)

- **"Make Love"**

  "Do You Wanna Make Love"—Peter McCann (1977)

  "Make Love To Your Mind"—Bill Withers (1976)

  "Makin' Love"—Climax Blues Band (1978)

  "Started Out Dancing, Ended Up Making Love"—Alan O'Day (1977)

- **Misc.**

  "Do Ya Wanna Get Funky With Me"—Peter Brown (1977)

  "Foxy Lady"—Crown Heights Affair (1976)

"Nice 'n' Naasty"—Salsoul Orchestra (1976)
"(Shake, Shake, Shake) Shake Your Booty"—K.C. and the
Sunshine Band (1976)

For sexual frankness, few could rival cock-rocker Ted Nugent, the man behind 1978's "Yank Me, Crank Me," but pop lust was generally confined to discos, where intoxicants, flashing lights, and mind-numbing volume made come-ons like Exile's "Kiss You All Over" seem almost subtle. Heck, even presidential hopeful Jimmy Carter was feeling a little randy. In a 1976 *Playboy* interview, Carter revealed he had "looked upon a lot of women with lust." The candidate's courageous revelations of virtual adultery were met with hypocritical derision from all sides, and helped distinguish him from incumbent/appointee Gerald Ford.

Meanwhile, the early seventies' gentler approach to sexual congress was still occasionally audible on catchphrase-derived records like Major Harris's "Laid Back Love," the Atlanta Rhythm Section's "So Into You," "Smokey Robinson's "Cruisin'," and the Jimmy Castor Bunch's "I Love a Mellow Groove." Recurring concepts included "Crazy Love" (Poco and the Allman Brothers) and "Easy" (Commodores and Keith Carradine).

At any other time, this surfeit of trendiness might have seemed a hopeless mess, and, indeed, for a while the late seventies appeared to have out-"Alley-Oop"ed the early sixties for sheer mercenary faddishness. But with "Another One Bites the Dust," "9 to 5," and "Physical" lying in wait just over the next rise, it was best to hold off a judgment like that, to use caution and skepticism, and to carry a copy of Howard J. Ruff's 1979 best-seller *How to Prosper During the Coming Bad Years.*

Family Feud

FLEETWOOD MAC

"Rhiannon (Will You Ever Win)" • Fleetwood Mac (Reprise, 1976)
"Say You Love Me" • Fleetwood Mac (Reprise, 1976)
"Go Your Own Way" • Fleetwood Mac (Warner Bros., 1977)
"Dreams" • Fleetwood Mac (Warner Bros., 1977)
"Don't Stop" • Fleetwood Mac (Warner Bros., 1977)
"You Make Loving Fun" • Fleetwood Mac (Warner Bros., 1977)
"Sentimental Lady" • Bob Welch (Capitol, 1977)
"Tusk" • Fleetwood Mac (Warner Bros., 1979)
"Sara" • Fleetwood Mac (Warner Bros., 1979)
"Gold" • John Stewart (RSO, 1979)

Supersonic commercial air travel began in 1976, but the year's most famous transatlantic sonic boom didn't come from the Concorde. That sound belonged to Fleetwood Mac, the 60/40 English/American ex-blues band whose twelfth (and second self-titled) album went to number one that year. "Soft-rock" FM was the emergent radio format, and *Fleetwood Mac*, with its blend of folk and rock influences, not to mention male and female voices, was the perfect fodder. The album became Warner Brothers' biggest seller ever (if briefly), with three singles, all Top Twenty, charting in *Billboard*. As it turned out, though, "Over My Head," "Rhiannon (Will You Ever Win)," and "Say You Love Me" were only the beginning.

The sessions for the album that would become *Rumours* (note the English spelling) began in late 1976 at a now legendary studio in Sausalito called the Record Plant. The record's working title, taken from the Christine McVie song (and future Bill Clinton campaign anthem) "Don't Stop," was *Yesterday's Gone,* and it was doubly appropriate: The old Fleetwood Mac—the one that had emerged from John Mayall's Bluesbreakers in 1967—was all but unrecognizable in the souped-up new platinum version, and all the current members' relationships were ending more or less simultaneously. The romantic travails of Mick Fleetwood, John and Christine McVie, and the American contingent, Stevie Nicks and Lindsey Buckingham, were becoming the stuff of legend, and the lengthy wait for the new album soon had media types and industry insiders trading gossip, hearsay, and, uh—

Rumours. John McVie's new idea for an album title struck the band as perfect: simple, ironic, mysterious. It was a nod to

the stories, some true, some laughable, that were circulating at the time. Yes, a tour had been postponed. Yes, production costs were soaring. Yes, tensions were high and the band was starring in what Buckingham has since called "a musical soap opera." But, contrary to what you might have heard in hushed tones over a Perrier water and avocado salad, there were no deaths, ménages à trois, séances, or fistfights.

Moreover, everything was fine in the musical department. The emotional turmoil, enough to destroy most other bands, had Fleetwood Mac peaking creatively. With songs like "Dreams" (Nicks's ticket to superstardom), "You Make Loving Fun" (Christine McVie's lush love letter to an unnamed other) and "Go Your Own Way" (Buckingham's aggressive farewell to Nicks) under way, the atmosphere was one of confidence, not disarray.

Well, okay, confident disarray. The *Rumours* master tapes were in danger of wearing out before the album was mixed, so numerous were the overdubs, and the exhausted, se-questered quintet was in a self-described "state of total weirdness," but the advance orders had climbed to 800,000 (another Warners record) and radio was clamoring for new material from Fleetwood and Company, now indisputably the Big Mac of the FM menu. Rock was high-level show business, and there was a lot more than artistic fulfillment riding on the new Fleetwood Mac album.

When *Rumours* was finally released in February 1977, it became an immediate fixture in the public consciousness, log-ging thirty-one weeks at number one, producing four Top Ten hits, winning the Grammy for Album of the Year, selling close to a million copies a week, and providing a cultural touch-stone for legions of disenfranchised post-Beatles pop fans. Even more than *Frampton Comes Alive!* or *Hotel California,* it was the record everybody—your friends, your relatives, your babysitter, even your teachers—seemed to have. Was it the best album of the decade? Not according to fans of Bob Marley, Joni Mitchell, or Peter Gabriel, but, then, what would they know about the cultural middle? *Rumours* was exactly as good as it needed to be. Its populist aesthetics, Good Witch of the West cover girl (Nicks), and contemporary relevance (the number of unmarried couples living together in the U.S. had more than doubled during the seventies, and divorces were up 60 percent) made it the perfect record for the *Mary Hartman, Mary Hartman* era. Call them Sly and the Dysfunctional Family Stone; the Mac were as contemporary as the IUD.

In the wake of *Rumours,* the band toured, appeared on magazine covers, accepted awards, and paired off romantically yet again—this time, Fleetwood and Nicks went their own way. Nicks and Buckingham participated in outside projects, including Walter Egan's "Magnet and Steel" and John Stewart's "Midnight Wind." Buckingham and Christine McVie were background vocalists on former Mac guitarist Bob Welch's mushy but beguiling "Sentimental Lady." The Macs had the Midas touch, much as Prince would in the mid-1980s, and the demands on their time, not to mention their spirits, were becoming extreme. Success begets pressure, and before long it was time for an encore.

If *Rumours* had been 1977's second-greatest clutch performance (let's give baseball's Reggie ["Mr. October"] Jackson his propers here), *Tusk* was 1979's most unexpected left turn. Stymied by multiplatinum expectations and creative differences, not to mention plain old burnout, Fleetwood Mac spent more than a million dollars and over a year making what amounted to their "white album": a sprawling, two-record document of a best-selling band going in many directions at once, with discrete contributions from individual members.

Buckingham, the band's de facto musical leader, had come under the influence of punk after seeing the Clash in England, and was intent on proving he wasn't a dinosaur (he did much of the basic tracking for his songs at his house, without input from the band). The title track featured a surreal cameo from the USC Trojan Marching Band, and the "Dreams"-style Stevie Nicks song "Sara" turned out to be the one truly radio-ready track in the four sides. Nevertheless, *Tusk* eventually sold into the millions, even at its inflated sixteen-dollar list price. ("Tusk," by the way, is a euphemism for the male member—see also "Sex Pistol.")

The late seventies, like the early sixties, was one of those disquieting periods during which rock and roll seems overly at home being a business. That means, among other things, that "(Shake, Shake, Shake) Shake Your Booty" is a latter-day "Loco-Motion," and that all sightings of Don Kirshner should be taken seriously. It also means that market-friendly periods get the pop stars they deserve, from Bobby Darin to Bobby Brown. Though originally a popular late-sixties blues-rock band, Fleetwood Mac will always be known for blockbuster audio like "Don't Stop"; their legacy is the streamlined, easy-to-own rock of the *Rumours* period. If that leaves them less respected than many of the acts they outsold, so be it; no one ever said life as a rich rock star was easy. Still, Fleetwood Mac was an outpost of vocal harmony in a period dominated by sometimes indulgent solo voices, and they managed to craft some mighty good pop songs amid considerable domestic chaos.

The Six Million Dollar Tan

WEST COAST POP

"Lowdown" • Boz Scaggs (Columbia, 1976)

"Popsicle Toes" • Michael Franks (Warner Bros., 1976)

"Baby Come Back" • Player (RSO, 1977)

"On and On" • Stephen Bishop (ABC, 1977)

"Whatcha Gonna Do?" • Pablo Cruise (A&M, 1977)

"Lonely Boy" • Andrew Gold (Asylum, 1977)

"I Just Wanna Stop" • Gino Vannelli (A&M, 1978)

"How Much I Feel" • Ambrosia (Warner Bros., 1978)

"What a Fool Believes" • The Doobie Brothers (Warner Bros., 1979)

"This Is It" • Kenny Loggins (Columbia, 1979)

California was governed by Ronald Reagan from 1966 to 1974, and again—in a broader sense—through two presidential terms in the eighties. In the intervening years (1975 to 1980), the "Have a Nice Day" state seemed a nation unto itself: a serene utopia full of young (or, anyway, youthful) singles stalking the perfect tan, and the perfect body, an impossibly clean machine powered by Perrier, granola, and what was then called "jogging." If that machine was also powered by greed, vanity, and cocaine, and if, as Woody Allen joked in *Annie Hall*, L.A.'s only cultural advantage was that you could turn right on a red light, it didn't seem to weigh heavily on the minds of Los Angelenos. Whether roller-skating along the boardwalk, following the Scarsdale Medical Diet, or seeking personal fulfillment through self-help gurus like Dr. Wayne

Dyer and Thomas Harris, the late-seventies Left Coaster was the embodiment of the Me Decade.

The soundtrack to this mellow scene was provided by blockbuster acts like Fleetwood Mac, Steely Dan, James Taylor, the Eagles, and Earth, Wind and Fire (all covered at length in other chapters), as well as Boz Scaggs, Linda Ronstadt, Jackson Browne, Steve Miller, and the post-biker Doobie Brothers. Though disparate in their origins and intentions, these artists shared a beguiling studio slickness and unfailing pop instincts: *Rumours, Aja, JT, All 'n All, Hotel California, Silk Degrees, Simple Dreams, Running On Empty, Fly Like an Eagle,* and *Minute by Minute* are among the best-selling albums of the late seventies. Heck, even the Dodgers were hot back then.

Boz Scaggs was the quintessence of West Coast cool, and "Lowdown," the out-of-nowhere 1976 smash with the skittering, funky bed track and so-light-it's-heavy flute line, was his masterstoke. One of four singles from *Silk Degrees* (not counting "We're All Alone," covered by both Rita Coolidge and Frankie Valli), "Lowdown" jibed perfectly with Scaggs's low-key, mirror-shades image; it made its case in measured, dulcet tones, never letting the emotion get out of hand. And it grooved like no Top Five single since Earth, Wind and Fire's "Shining Star." (Boz declined to have the song included on the 25 million–selling *Saturday Night Fever* soundtrack: oops.)

Like many of the best of the West, "Lowdown" poked holes in the ultra-hip L.A. scene while reveling in its shiny surface. It may be illusory and dangerous, went the logic, but, damn, it makes you wanna strut your stuff! "Hollywood," from Scaggs's less popular but equally good follow-up LP, *Down Two Then Left,* applied the same approach to a budding starlet. Other locally relevant hits of the day included "Hot Child in the

City," Nick Gilder's ode to a Hollywood Boulevard hooker; "Honey Don't Leave L.A.," James Taylor's attack on a fast-tracking girlfriend; "Peg," Steely Dan's love/hate letter to a showbiz ingenue; "White Punks on Dope," the Tubes' hilarious take on Hollywood bratdom; and almost anything from *Hotel California.*

The Doobie Brothers, the SoCal boogie band already famous for future classic-rock fodder like "Long Train Runnin'," entered a new phase when singer-songwriter Michael McDonald (just cut from the ever-shrinking Steely Dan roster) joined in 1976. McDonald brought not only a distinctively percussive approach to keyboards and a way with melody, but one of the most unforgettable white soul voices in the history of pop. "Takin' It to the Streets," from the platinum album of the same name, began a string of hits that climaxed with 1979's Grammy-gobbling "Minute by Minute." During those years, McDonald was omnipresent; while crafting hit after hit for his band, he also wrote or performed with Carly Simon, Nicolette Larson, Bonnie Raitt, Steely Dan, and Kenny Loggins.

The McDonald-Loggins songwriting partnership was fruitful for both artists. Though it was Loggins who first recorded "What a Fool Believes" (his 1978 version is an undiscovered gem), it was "This Is It," a plea to his ailing father, that cemented his position as an equal partner. The Bob James–produced *Celebrate Me Home* (1977) is probably the best of Loggins's post–Loggins and Messina solo albums, coming as it did before Loggins began dabbling with "rock" ("Danger Zone," indeed).

Among L.A.'s other pop writers–in–residence were Michael Franks, the former English-lit major whose musical dirty jokes ("Popsicle Toes") put the *"forn"* in "California"; Stephen Bishop, the movie-theme specialist whose excellent 1976 album *Careless* spawned the hit "On and On"; and Gino

Vannelli, the transplanted Montrealer who scaled his epic ambitions down to size on his breakthrough 1978 album, *Brother to Brother*. Newcomers like Pablo Cruise ("Whatcha Gonna Do?"), Andrew Gold ("Lonely Boy"), Player ("Baby Come Back"), and the Sanford-Townsend Band ("Smoke from a Distant Fire") staked out California pop's middle ground, while serious writers like Randy Newman, Warren Zevon, Rickie Lee Jones, and Tom Waits flourished in spite of their picture-postcard surroundings. Frank Zappa, Sparks, and the Tubes played left field.

The bustling scene witnessed technological breakthroughs (Ry Cooder's *Bop Till You Drop* was the first digitally-recorded LP); stylistic innovations (Zappa's post-Varèse rock, Jones's post-Bernstein pop plainsong); even social conscience—the MUSE Concerts for a Non-Nuclear Future (immortalized on a 1979 triple album) featured much of the West Coast musical mafia, including Cooder, Browne, Taylor, the Doobie Brothers, Poco, Raitt, and Larson. The party was effectively over by the time of the great Christopher Cross too-many-Grammys debacle of 1981—not to mention the almost simultaneous breakups of Steely Dan, the Eagles, and the Doobies—but while it lasted, the California sound helped to define the feel-good ethos of the well-funded seventies, and left behind a Corvette convertible full of bitchin' pop tunes.

The Chain: California Pop's Old-Dude Network

Jackson Browne produces **Warren Zevon** . . . whose "Poor Poor Pitiful Me" is covered by **Linda Ronstadt** . . . whose backup band becomes the **Eagles,** who cover "Ol' 55" by **Tom Waits,** who is romantically linked to **Rickie Lee Jones** . . . whose "Easy Money" is covered by Little Feat founder **Lowell George,** who produces *Shakedown Street* by the **Grateful Dead** . . . whose *Terrapin Station* is produced by Keith

Olsen, producer of **Fleetwood Mac** . . . whose Stevie Nicks duets on "Whenever I Call You 'Friend'" with **Kenny Loggins,** who co-writes "What a Fool Believes" with the **Doobie Brothers' Michael McDonald,** who is a former member of **Steely Dan** . . . whose later albums feature guitarist **Larry Carlton,** who is a former member of the **Crusaders,** who are featured on *Sleeping Gypsy* by **Michael Franks** . . . whose albums feature saxophonist **David Sanborn,** who also plays on "How Sweet It Is to Be Loved By You" by **James Taylor,** who is produced by **Peter Asher,** who also produces *The Glow* by **Bonnie Raitt,** who performs at the M.U.S.E. concerts . . . which also features **Ry Cooder,** who plays on *Sail Away* by **Randy Newman** . . . whose *Born Again* features **the Eagles** . . . whose **Joe Walsh** produces *Souvenirs* by **Dan Fogelberg,** who guests on albums by **Jackson Browne,** who co-writes "Take It Easy" with **the Eagles** . . . whose mid-seventies lineup includes **Randy Meisner,** who is a former member of **Poco** . . . whose **Jim Messina** records seven albums with partner **Kenny Loggins,** who is a charter member of **Gator Creek** . . . whose **Michael Omartian** plays piano on "Aja" by **Steely Dan** . . . whose former drummer **Jeff Porcaro** later joins **Toto** . . . whose members back **Boz Scaggs,** who is a former bandmate of **Steve Miller,** who has a hit entitled "Heart Like a Wheel" which is also the title of an album by **Linda Ronstadt,** who covers "Willin'" by **Lowell George,** who, as mentioned, covers "Easy Money" by **Rickie Lee Jones** . . . whose debut album features saxophonist **Tom Scott,** who also plays on *Aja* by **Steely Dan** . . . whose alumni include **Doobie Brothers** guitarist **Jeff "Skunk" Baxter,** who produces **Livingston Taylor,** who is the younger brother of **James Taylor** . . . whose "Her Town Too" is a duet with **J.D. Souther,** who is a former member of **Longbranch Pennywhistle,** a band which also featured **Glenn Frey** . . . whose **Eagles** partner **Don Henley's** "Desperado" is covered by **Linda Ronstadt** . . . whose backup vocalists include **Nicolette Larson,** who duets on "Let Me Go, Love" with **Michael McDonald** . . . whose "It Keeps You Runnin'" is covered by **Carly Simon,** who is married to **James Taylor** . . . whose touring band includes pianist **Bill Payne** of **Little Feat** . . . whose **Lowell George** is a former bandmate of **Frank Zappa** . . . whose opening acts include **Tom Waits,** who . . . Well, you get the idea.

A Little Bit Country, a Little Bit Rock and Roll

THE EAGLES

"Take It to the Limit" • Eagles (Asylum, 1976)
"New Kid in Town" • Eagles (Asylum, 1976)
"Everything You Did" • Steely Dan (ABC, 1976)
"Hotel California" • Eagles (Asylum, 1977)
Life in the Fast Lane" • Eagles (Asylum, 1977)
Life's Been Good" • Joe Walsh (Asylum, 1978)
"Heartache Tonight" • Eagles (Asylum, 1979)
"The Long Run" • Eagles (Asylum, 1979)
"Crazy Love" • Poco (ABC, 1979)
"You're Only Lonely" • J. D. Souther (Columbia, 1979)

E ven by the inflated standards of the "bigger is better" era, the Eagles were huge. *Eagles Greatest Hits 1971–1975* was the first album ever to "go platinum." *Hotel California* topped the charts four separate times. All told, from 1976 to 1979, the band named for America's mascot sold over 40 million albums.

The largesse of the Eagles' largeness was the all-access party pass it afforded the band. The "third encore," as their perpetual after-show bender was dubbed, was more than just sex, drugs, and country-rock: Lear jets, Château Lafite Roth-schild, and occasional visits from Stevie Nicks were also part of the package. Eagles co-founder Glenn Frey has said, "Led Zeppelin might argue with us, but I think we had the greatest traveling party of the seventies." Don Henley, for his part, considered the "third encore" a predictable reaction to being young, rich, and famous. (Bassist Randy Meisner left the band in 1977, citing exhaustion; you'd be tired, too, if you'd outpartied Zep.)

In the parlance of the time, the boys were partying hearty, and because they did it with one eagle-eye open, excess became raw material for success (see diagram). *Hotel California* (1976), a best-selling almost-concept album about the dark underside of the platinum lifestyle, addressed the perils of decadence (the title track), drug abuse ("Life in the Fast Lane"), and the fickle nature of celebrity ("New Kid in Town") with dead-on, crafty couplets. But *Ho-Cal* was more than just a musical journal entry; it was a meticulously crafted masterstroke from a band that, as it turned out, couldn't do much

THE CIRCLE OF (Night) Life:
How the Eagles became their own best critics

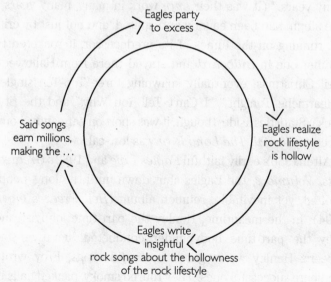

Eagles party to excess

Eagles realize rock lifestyle is hollow

Eagles write insightful rock songs about the hollowness of the rock lifestyle

Said songs earn millions, making the ...

better (Bob Seger once remarked that the Eagles broke up because the album was impossible to top).

Ho-Cal tracks like Joe Walsh's "Pretty Maids All in a Row" and Randy Meisner's "Try and Love Again" were evidence of the Eagles' democratic streak: Henley and Frey, in the Lennon-and-McCartney tradition ("Hey, let's let George write one!") occasionally stepped aside for other band members. But "Hotel California"—the band's "Stairway to Heaven"—easily outshone the surrounding material, even going to number one at its original, sprawling album length. (Footnote: The song's reference to "steely knives" was a tip of the hat to Steely Dan, who had mentioned the Eagles a few months earlier in "Everything You Did.") "Life in the Fast Lane," with its satirical edge and power guitar, foreshadowed future Henley hits like "Dirty Laundry."

The labored followup to *Ho-Cal* was 1979's *The Long Run,* a disappointment in spite of *Rolling Stone* critic Timothy White's assessment of it as "the Eagles' best work in many, many years." (It was their *only* work in many, many years.) The album had been eagerly anticipated, and not just by critics: running on the fumes of its predecessor, it rocketed to number one in *Billboard* and stayed there from Halloween until Christmas, eventually spawning three Top-Ten singles ("Heartache Tonight," "I Can't Tell You Why," and the title track). Statistics aside, though, it was short on ear candy; compared to *Ho-Cal, The Long Run* was low-cal.

After 1980's eerily faithful *Eagles Live* and 1982's *Greatest Hits, Volume 2,* the Eagles shut down until the long–pooh-poohed, yet inevitable, reunion album (*Hell Freezes Over,* 1994). In the meantime, Henley the part-time lobbyist and Frey the part-time bodybuilder conducted lucrative solo careers: Henley wrote good successful songs, Frey wrote mediocre successful ones. They toured smoky, packed halls in support of crowd-pleasing albums like *Building the Perfect Beast* and *The Allnighter,* and, at times, it must have felt like nothing had changed. But something had changed, something essential: Don and Glenn, the late seventies' wildest party animals, had learned to call it a night. After the second encore.

Artificial Heart

CORPORATE ROCK

"More Than a Feeling" • Boston (Epic, 1976)
"Feels Like the First Time" • Foreigner (Atlantic, 1977)
"Barracuda" • Heart (Portrait, 1977)
"Carry On Wayward Son" • Kansas (Kirshner, 1977)
"Come Sail Away" • Styx (A&M, 1977)
"Paradise by the Dashboard Light" • Meat Loaf (Epic, 1978)
"Hold the Line" • Toto (Columbia, 1978)
"Lovin', Touchin', Squeezin'" • Journey (Columbia, 1979)
"Heartbreaker" • Pat Benatar (Chrysalis, 1979)
"Hold On" • Triumph (RCA, 1979)

In 1978, just two years after Soviet surgeons implanted the first artificial heart into a living being (a calf), Steve Perry (a singer) landed a job with Journey (a band). The twenty-nine-year-old Perry was expert at the fine art of feigned emotion—of artificial heart, if you will—and it wasn't long before Journey became a key cog in the well-oiled machine called corporate rock. Like the "no-name" generic products that had just begun appearing in North American supermarkets, corporate rock bands quickly established a niche in the marketplace. Journey, for one, enjoyed a string of seventeen Top 40 hits beginning in 1979, changing the course of rock history not one iota, but providing a vocal paradigm for their peers: for a while it seemed every mainstream rocker was singing like Perry. (This was a few years before every mainstream rocker began singing like [Bryan] Ferry.)

Journey was a model late-seventies corporate rock band—the genre's poster children. Except, of course, that not many Top 40 listeners would have recognized them on a poster, one of the chief characteristics of corporate rock bands being the members' anonymity. Rarely photographed for album covers, corp-rockers opted instead for van-friendly graphics by an army of post–Roger Dean illustrators. The musicians, when they were visible, favored wide collars, tight jeans, and long, limp, lifeless hair (call them the anti-Farrahs).

Corporate rock bands lurked behind their carefully chosen band names, which almost always consisted of a single word perfect for snappy logo designs like Boston's spaceship, Toto's dagger, and Heart's heart. (Solo artists were exceptions to this rule, with their innovative use of two-word combinations like "Pat" and "Benatar," "Meat" and "Loaf.") For consumers, the logos represented the promise of consistency, the comfort of a known quantity. As another member of America's corporate community boasted, "The best surprise is no surprise."

Inside the slick packages, listeners found soulless studio concoctions that relied less on rock-and-roll muscle than on market research. With ballads edgy enough for AOR (album-oriented rock) stations and rock tunes polished enough for CHR (contemporary hit radio) stations, the bands sought to please a broad consumer base while pandering to newly inflexible radio formats. Journey's "Lovin', Touchin', Squeezin'" (1979), while invoking rock's decades-old preoccupation with heavy petting, felt coldly calculated, lacking the true lust that had informed early-seventies cock-rock classics like "Brown Sugar" and "Rock and Roll Hoochie Koo."

The rock-by-number approach, then, was short on cheap

thrills, but long on commercial clout; like Apple Computer (founded in April 1976), corporate rock's financial situation had improved steadily since 1976, the year Boston's spaceship insignia landed on the music scene with a multiplatinum thud. Propelled by the massive success of the fist-pumping Top-Ten anthem "More Than a Feeling" (even Morris Albert's "Feelings" had more feeling), *Boston* was archetypal corporate rock. Carefully constructed by Tom Scholz, a former product designer for Polaroid, the album was anything but "instamatic"; Scholz was notorious for taking his time in the studio. Indeed, no one could accuse Boston of flooding the market (their first three albums, *Boston, Don't Look Back,* and *Third Stage,* were released over a span of ten years), but whereas studio hounds like Steely Dan and Paul Simon ultimately justified their endless tinkering, Scholz's work had a sameness that belied all the well-publicized time and effort. Nevertheless, "More Than a Feeling," an orgy of double-tracked bluster that sounded more like a seconded motion than a response to the Muses, became corporate rock's theme song, and Boston its parent company. (Scholz's most important legacy to musicians is probably the Rockman, a portable studio gizmo that, over the years, saved many a guitarist from lugging an amp to a recording session.)

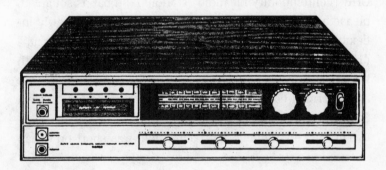

Foreigner, led by former A&R man Mick Jones (*not* the one from the Clash), were corporate rockers as well, despite a musical ancestry that included sixties Brit-rock bands like Spooky Tooth and King Crimson. They had a one-word, logo-friendly name, a bombastic singer (Lou Gramm), bland hard-rock songs featuring otherwise spicy subject matter ("Feels Like the First Time," "Hot Blooded," "Dirty White Boy"), and band members whose recognizability factor was so low that, in the event of their disappearance, reliable sketches would have been hard to come by.

Kansas and Styx adhered to the corporate code as well, but were more obviously influenced by progressive rock than their peers. Prior to Kansas's breakthrough ("Carry On Wayward Son") in 1977, the band had been a rare example of pure Stateside prog rock. Success on the AM dial, however, seemed to dim their musical ambitions somewhat, and Kansas soon joined the grand parade of lifeless packaging. Styx, hailing from Chicago (already in use as a band name), first cracked the charts in 1975 with "Lady," an insufferable power ballad that became the blueprint for 1979's "Babe." The band's "Come Sail Away" (1977), a multisectioned stadium rocker on a near-biblical scale ("a gathering of angels appeared above our heads"), doesn't deserve to be mentioned in the same sentence with "Stairway to Heaven," but it shared with the Zep classic not only heavenly imagery, but a confounding dance-floor challenge: Both tracks started as "slow songs" and built to big climaxes, catching slow-dancing adolescents in rhythmic collapse as they refused to separate. Other prog-rock/corp-rock crossover acts included ELO, Starcastle, and the Alan Parsons Project.

Marvin Lee Aday ("Meat Loaf" to you) was fresh from a stint with Ted Nugent and a role in the cult movie *The Rocky Horror Picture Show* when he recorded "Paradise by the

Dashboard Light," his 1978 epic about a backseat teen romance. The cornerstone of the best-selling Todd Rundgren–
produced *Bat Out of Hell* album, "Paradise" took the age-old
baseball-as-sex metaphor to a new level by featuring the voice
of New York Yankees announcer (and former Yankee short-
stop) Phil Rizzuto. (Despite the fact that it stalled at number
39 on the Billboard chart, "Paradise" was more memorable,
and inspired more atonal sing-alongs, than *Bat Out Of Hell*'s
biggest hit, "Two Out of Three Ain't Bad.")

Although most corporate rock came from one big generic
soup—Triumph's "Hold On" is a good example—female acts
like Heart and Pat Benatar at least distinguished themselves
by crashing the all-male party at Corprock, Inc. They paved
the way for female-fronted eighties acts like Alannah Myles
and Starship and, because they had *way* better hair, you
could tell they weren't Boston. In the end, though, songs like
Heart's "Crazy On You" and Benatar's "Heartbreaker" did little
to stretch corporate rock's well-marked boundaries.

Toto, the band of Los Angeles studio musicians that had
given Boz Scaggs's *Silk Degrees* (1976) much of its sleek,
funky spirit, entered the fray themselves in 1978 with "Hold
the Line." While notable because it was the only corporate
rock song ever to actually swing, "Hold the Line" unfortunately laid the groundwork for a musically distinguished but
stylistically handcuffed career. Toto's extracurricular pursuits
included Steely Dan, Michael Jackson, Marc Jordan, and the
Tubes.

Shockingly, corporate rock outlived punk, the genre in-
vented to erase it. Journey, Boston, Foreigner, and Heart all
scored their biggest hits in the eighties, and new bands like
Def Leppard, REO Speedwagon, and Loverboy emerged to
keep the flame (more like a pilot light) alive. In the late seventies, with major labels swallowing their competitors (EMI

bought UA, MCA bought ABC), robots assembling cars, and babies being born from test tubes, corporate rock had made a kind of sick sense. But in the wake of the Clash and the Sex Pistols, it simply smelled like unrepentant commerce, its biggest hits increasingly indistinguishable from commercial jingles; it was, after all, the first musical genre ever named for its earning power.

Today, listening to "vintage" corporate rock for any length of time conjures a storybook collection of faceless tin men crying "oil can," a band of formulaic Foreigners in the Land of Oz on a futile Journey to find a Heart. As they march along the winding road—did we mention it's paved with gold?—they survey the barren, almost lunar, landscape. "Toto," they whisper, "I don't think we're in Kansas anymore."

Bicentennial Blues

BRUCE SPRINGSTEEN

"Tenth Avenue Freeze-Out" • Bruce Springsteen (Columbia, 1976)
"Blinded by the Light" • Manfred Mann's Earth Band (Warner Bros., 1976)
"Prove It All Night" • Bruce Springsteen (Columbia, 1978)
"Badlands" • Bruce Springsteen (Columbia, 1978)
"Darkness on the Edge of Town" • Bruce Springsteen (Columbia, 1978)
"Candy's Room" • Bruce Springsteen (Columbia, 1978)
"Racing in the Street" • Bruce Springsteen (Columbia, 1978)
"Because the Night" • Patti Smith Group (Arista, 1978)
"Streets of Fire" • Bruce Springsteen (Columbia, 1978)
"Fire" • Pointer Sisters (Planet, 1978)

TITLE: "MAY 1972"
INT. PARKING GARAGE. NIGHT.

Leaning over the hood of a car, BRUCE signs the first long-term management deal of his career. (It's a soon-to-be-infamous arrangement [representing "unconscionable exploitation," according to a 1976 independent auditor's report] with Laurel Canyon Productions, the management company headed by MIKE APPEL and JIM CRETECOS.) When he has finished, BRUCE looks up at his new managers, unable to suppress a smile.

The preceding New York minute may sound like the preposterous opening scene of a made-for-cable Bruce Springsteen biopic, but it's actually how it went down. In retrospect, the parking lot provides good symbolic context: First, the contract was literally signed in the dark, suggesting an inability to read the fine print; second, our hero, king of the road-as-escape metaphor, signed on the hood of a car.

In 1976, four years older and engaged in a legal battle to wriggle free, Springsteen had come to consider the Laurel Canyon deal more ambush than escape. But in 1972, the artist, not yet "the Boss" (as his royalty statements would soon make clear), must have felt like he was doing eighty with the wind in his hair when, the day after signing his deal, Appel and Company landed him an audition at Columbia Records with John Hammond, the veteran producer who had signed Billie Holiday and Bob Dylan.

The 1998 Springsteen CD boxed set, *Tracks,* begins with that historic four-song audition. The first voice you hear is the unintentionally comical monotone of John Hammond, unaware he's on the brink of the second-biggest signing of his career. The four unadorned songs that follow, each of which wound up on Springsteen's debut album, barely hint at the rollicking, R&B-tinged epics that would eventually constitute *Greetings from Asbury Park, NJ* (1973); *The Wild, the Innocent and the E. Street Shuffle* (1973); and the near-perfect *Born to Run* (1975).

The lopsided nature of his management deal became clear to Springsteen when he received a royalty statement from Laurel Canyon Productions in May 1976. The artist had brought in more than $2 million over the first four years of his management contract, but the statement amounted to just $67,000—for the entire period. In the four years leading up to that fiscal slap in the face, Springsteen had signed with Columbia; earned a reputation for unforgettable live performances; been hailed as "rock and roll's future" by critic Jon

Landau; become rock and roll's present, with three critically acclaimed and successively better selling albums (*Born to Run* went to number 3); and landed on the covers of *Time* and *Newsweek* during the same week in October 1975. The star-maker machinery was in overdrive. It's no wonder Springsteen's paltry take gave him pause.

At the peak of his career, then, Springsteen found himself in a legal imbroglio that would keep him from recording for a full year. The unfortunate sabbatical ultimately resulted in a three-year gap between albums, enough time to inspire a few "Where is he now?" columns (in the mid-seventies, an album a year was considered the minimum). Despite his silence, Springsteen maintained his profile with occasional shows and his growing exploits as a songwriter. "Tenth Avenue Freeze-Out," the funky final single from *Born to Run*, had recently—inexplicably—stiffed at number 83, but a slick cover of "Blinded by the Light" (originally from *Asbury Park*), by Manfred Mann's Earth Band, went to number one, sparking debate about that "douche" line (it's actually "cut loose like a *deuce*"). It wouldn't be the last Springsteen cover of the late seventies: Mann also recorded *Asbury Park*'s "Spirit in the Night"; the Pointer Sisters took "Fire" (then unrecorded by Springsteen) to number 2; and "Because the Night," written with Patti Smith, turned out to be the punk diva's only hit.

Springsteen resumed recording in May 1977 after settling out of court. Laurel Canyon escaped with a handsome payoff, Springsteen with the freedom to renegotiate with Columbia, and to reenter the studio with his producer of choice, the aforementioned Jon Landau. Landau would be promoted to manager a year later, but for now, the two set about recording Springsteen's only late-seventies album, the downbeat *Darkness on the Edge of Town*.

Though overshadowed (to this day) by its more expansive

predecessor, *Darkness* was a minor masterpiece; in retrospect, a bridge linking the epic ambitions of *Born to Run* to the leaner sounds of *The River* (1980) and *Nebraska* (1982). Lyrically, its focus was blue-collar America. On the slump-shouldered "Racing In the Streets," Springsteen's description of the working-class antihero's car ("a 'sixty-nine Chevy with a three-ninety-six") sounded positively funereal. On the pulsar-brilliant title track, a descendant of Johnny Rivers's "Poor Side of Town," the almost mumbled verse was interrupted by one of the most memorable snare shots in rock history, a Max Weinberg whack that sets up Springsteen's gloriously vengeful invitation to the wrong side of the tracks. (*Darkness*'s grim tone meant party songs like "Give the Girl a Kiss" and "So Young and in Love" [later included on *Tracks*] had to be shelved.)

Springsteen was still able to imagine something beyond the darkness, but the possibilities for his characters were starting to dwindle. On "Candy's Room," the narrator's only escape was into the arms of a hooker. On "Prove It All Night" (the album's only hit), the lovers put on a show of optimism, clinging to a shaky-at-best criminal nobility. On "The Promised Land," our hapless hero drives straight into a twister that's ready to "blow everything down that ain't got the faith to stand its ground." For the first time, Springsteen had begun painting his characters into corners. Take "Factory": in an era of record-setting foreign-car sales in the U.S., and concurrent record-setting domestic losses by Chrysler, the Silkwood-esque workers walking through the factory gates "with death in their eyes" were truly without prospects.

A rock-and-roll Rocky whose compassion for the little guy had now become central to his popularity, Springsteen would see his audience grow in the years following *Darkness*. Fueled as ever by cathartic, marathon concerts and climaxing with 1984's multiplatinum *Born in the U.S.A.* (whose title track was infamously coopted by Ronald Reagan), his star would continue to rise until he disbanded the E Street Band (named after a street in Belmar, New Jersey) in 1989 and retreated into more personal, intimate recordings. He once said, "If the price of fame is that you have to be isolated from the people you write for . . . that's too fuckin' high a price to pay." Which brings to mind a certain Tupelo, Mississippi-born, King, and another scene for the Boss biopic.

TITLE: "APRIL 29, 1976"
EXT. GRACELAND MANSION. NIGHT.

BRUCE scales the wall of the PRESLEY compound. Apprehended by a SECURITY GUARD, he is unceremoniously ejected from the grounds. The isolated, bloated target of BRUCE's bizarre pilgrimage does not appear.

Maybe on that early Memphis morning, Springsteen was trying to gauge the extent to which Elvis had lost touch with his fans. Maybe he wanted a "this could happen to me" wake-up call. By 1976, the price of fame for Elvis had long ago become "too fuckin' high."

Logical Songs

PROGRESSIVE POP

"Love Is the Drug" • Roxy Music (Atco, 1976)

"Bohemian Rhapsody" • Queen (Elektra, 1976)

"Dream Weaver" • Gary Wright (Warner Bros., 1976)

"The Things We Do for Love" • 10cc (Mercury, 1977)

"Year of the Cat" • Al Stewart (Janus, 1977)

"Solsbury Hill" • Peter Gabriel (Atco, 1977)

"I Wouldn't Want to Be Like You" • Alan Parsons Project (Arista, 1977)

"Telephone Line" • Electric Light Orchestra (Jet, 1977)

"The Logical Song" • Supertramp (A&M, 1979)

"The Man with the Child in His Eyes" • Kate Bush (EMI, 1979)

By the end of 1976, progressive rock was on the skids. Peter Gabriel had left Genesis, Rick Wakeman had left Yes, Godley and Creme had left 10cc, King Crimson had disbanded, Roxy Music and the Moody Blues were on hiatus, David Bowie was making soul music, and the Electric Light Orchestra was morphing into the Bee Gees. The conventional wisdom of the early seventies—that rock was serious, had outgrown its roots, and was *progressing* toward some pseudo-classical nirvana—was being refuted on all sides by (among others) KISS, disco, and Peter Frampton. Sales of albums dealing with kings, wizards, jolly Olde England, and, like, other planets, were on the decline.

Only a few years earlier, prog rock had seemed an unstoppable commercial force: 1972 was the year of Yes's *Fragile* and the accompanying hit "Roundabout"; 1973 was the year of Jethro Tull's *A Passion Play* (number one in the U.S.) and Pink Floyd's *Dark Side of the Moon* (29 million sold, 741 weeks on the *Billboard* album chart). As late as 1974, the bombastic trio Emerson, Lake and Palmer had merited, at least in the opinion of their record company, a *three*-LP live album: *Welcome Back My Friends, to the Show That Never Ends—Ladies and Gentlemen, Emerson, Lake and Palmer.*

But from 1976 onward, orthodox progressive rock waned; that is, the sprawling, moody electronic suites that had fueled FM rock radio during the early seventies disappeared, or sold poorly, anyway. With the exception of Pink Floyd, whose two late-seventies albums continued the band's multiplatinum pace, most of the epic-mongers of the Nixon era were forced to downscale. (Those who didn't experienced that sinking, dinosaurs-on-ice feeling: Gentle Giant's 1977 double live LP, *Playing the Fool,* found the influential band treading water, and ELP's *Works* mostly didn't.)

Into the void created by prog rock's misfortunes sailed a host of new, milder "serious" bands, whose humor (Queen), pop smarts (Supertramp), and style (Roxy Music, mach two) would ensure their survival into the eighties. Stylistic descendants of the Beatles, they met the melodic requirements of AM radio while still producing thoughtful, original work. This new, leaner breed of pomp rock deserves a name—let's call it "progressive pop."

Genesis, recently deserted by its gifted frontman Peter Gabriel, regrouped and slowly but surely built a mass audience: *A Trick of the Tail* (1976) adapted Gabriel's methods to the four-minute rock song; *Wind and Wuthering* (1977), though slightly more epic in proportion, spawned a minor hit in "Your Own Special Way"; the post–Steve Hackett *And*

Then There Were Three (1978) spawned a bigger hit in "Follow You, Follow Me"; and, before long, Phil Collins had the whole outfit bopping like a blueblood Earth, Wind and Fire. Does that mean late-seventies Genesis is without merit? Not if "Ripples" *(Trick)*, "Blood on the Rooftops" *(Wind)*, and "Undertow" *(Three)* are any indication. The band's methods simply fit their time.

The same was true of Supertramp, the hardworking, Wurlitzer-hammering London quintet whose hook-filled, fastidiously arranged *Crime of the Century* had been a U.K. number one in 1975. More pop than rock, more Lennon-McCartney than Waters-Gilmour, Supertramp's two singer-songwriters, Roger Hodgson and Richard Davies, worked up a serious head of creative steam on the albums that followed (*Crisis? What Crisis?* and *Even in the Quietest Moments . . .*), finally striking platinum with *Breakfast in America* (1979). The chart-topping *Breakfast*—which included the hits "Goodbye Stranger," "Take the Long Way Home," and "The Logical Song"—was unworthy of all the attention, especially in light of its predecessors, but if you were hoping we'd slag Supertramp like all the other Captain Beefheart–loving rock critics, you bought the wrong book. We will say this: After *Paris,* the obligatory trophy double live LP, the golden age of 'Tramp was over.

Roxy Music, on the other hand, was just getting started. Increasingly a vessel for Bryan Ferry's decadent romantic fantasies, the band began reaching a larger (read: American) audience in 1976 when "Love Is the Drug," an ode to the late-seventies singles scene, went to number 30 in *Billboard* (for quintessential late Roxy, see *Flesh + Blood* [1980] or *Avalon* [1982]). Queen, aka *The Freddie Mercury Show,* put everything they knew into the campy, overdub-happy rock operetta "Bohemian Rhapsody" (1976), and promptly went on a commercial tear that didn't really end until after "Rhapsody" rode the *Wayne's World* juggernaut to number 2 again in 1992.

Among prog pop's other hitmakers: former *Abbey Road* engineer Alan Parsons, softsung pop auteur Al Stewart (produced by Parsons), Spooky Tooth co-founder Gary Wright, high-achieving Beatlemaniacs 10cc, and lapsed classical rockers ELO (twelve Top 40 hits, 1976–79). (Also of note: Brian Eno, Be-Bop Deluxe, City Boy, Crack the Sky, Hawkwind, Kansas, U.K., Renaissance, Saga, Synergy, and Starcastle— this last being a technically accomplished Columbia signing so stilted they made Yes sound like a soul act.)

Peter Gabriel took two years off after leaving Genesis before launching his solo career, but after that kept up a dizzying pace. His first three albums (all eponymously titled) revealed a versatility that even *The Lamb Lies Down on Broadway* (1974) had barely hinted at. "Solsbury Hill," the folkiest 7/4 of the rock era, documented, in highly symbolic language, the artist's decision to leave his former band. "D.I.Y." hinted, lyrically and musically, at the pared-down days to come, "Family Snapshot" put listeners inside the mind of an assassin, "Excuse Me" was a sardonic barbershop-quartet ditty, and the gorgeous "Humdrum" outlushed Genesis. Today, Gabriel is the foremost proponent of rock artsong.

ELP singer-guitarist Greg Lake (known to the world as "L") once said, "European musicians tend to come from a classical heritage, American musicians tend to come from a blues-based heritage," and though there are exceptions (John Mayall, Eric Carmen), truer words were never spoken. The pseudo-classical bent of most British and European progressive bands is the reason they seldom are accorded rock-and-roll legitimacy by critics—the line from Chuck Berry to Jethro Tull is a wobbly one indeed—but once you clear away the

Spinal Tap–style production numbers and pseudo-Tolkien storytelling, there really is some rock there, bluesy or no.

Progressive pop's crowning glory was Pink Floyd's *The Wall*, released on the eve of the eighties. A Roger Waters–penned concept album about "how the futile scramble for material things obscures our possible path to understanding," as well as (like *Wish You Were Here*) the indignities of being a rock star, it eventually sold 10 million copies in the U.S.; became a hit movie; and launched two hits, "Run Like Hell" and "Another Brick in the Wall (Part Two)"—backup vocals courtesy of students from the Islington Green School. It also marked the end of rock's classical period, Queensrÿche notwithstanding. What followed—the metal- and MTV-dominated 1980s—was enough to make one (well, us, anyway) nostalgic for prog rock's excesses. Keith Emerson's *Piano Concerto No. 1* was at least ambitious; *Asia* was just a highly polished turd.

Future Legend

DAVID BOWIE

"Golden Years" • David Bowie (RCA, 1975)
"TVC 15" • David Bowie (RCA, 1976)
"Stay" • David Bowie (RCA, 1976)
"Station to Station" • David Bowie (RCA, 1976)
"Sound and Vision" • David Bowie (RCA, 1977)
"Be My Wife" • David Bowie (RCA, 1977)
"Beauty and the Beast" • David Bowie (RCA, 1977)
"Lust for Life" • Iggy Pop (RCA, 1977)
"Heroes" • David Bowie (RCA, 1978)
"D.J." • David Bowie (RCA, 1978)

For a world-famous, multimillion-selling pop star, David Bowie (1970s edition) had his share of abstract tendencies. He used extravagant, theatrical sets, flirted with German Expressionism and nonlinear writing techniques, and calculatingly coopted existing pop-music styles for his own arty purposes (he probably felt as passionate about glam rock, for example, as Andy Warhol did about Campbell's soup). His reassemblage of Western culture's flotsam and jetsam into compelling new visions was nothing short of miraculous, and his public statements ("Rock stardom comes down to the cut of your trousers") were not the thoughts of a traditional teen idol. Still, Bowie never came up with anything as downright weird as his appearance with Iggy Pop on *The Dinah Shore Show.*

It was April 1977. Bowie's seminal album *Low* had been out since January, and his production of Iggy Pop's *The Idiot* was about to reignite the former Stooges frontman's career. The pair had recently returned from working in West Germany, and at that dark hour in history (the number one song in the world was ABBA's "Dancing Queen"), they definitely represented the pop-cultural far left. Thus it was a little trippy to see them visiting with daytime talk-show host, former big-band chanteuse, and golf-tournament namesake Dinah Shore. Yes, Bowie would later duet with Bing Crosby on "The Little Drummer Boy" (on Crosby's 1977 Christmas special), and narrate *Peter and the Wolf* for RCA Classics, but the whole tableau was surreal.

Bowie no doubt loved the incongruity—it's what he had trafficked in since launching "Major Tom" into the wild black yonder on 1969's *Space Oddity*. He was both devoted husband and bisexual libertine, aesthete and hard-rocker, serenader and satirist. Lost in the multimedia madness, however, were his prodigious skills as a songwriter. During his prime—let's say, 1972–77—he produced a body of work that rivals any in the rock era. Even beyond signature tunes like "Changes," "Suffragette City," and "Rebel Rebel," he seemed capable of summoning an album's worth of brilliant material at will, so much so that songs good enough to represent the core of any other artist's catalog were peripheral to Bowie's. One good example is "We Are the Dead," a *Diamond Dogs* track full of both dread *and* melody (goth bands, take note), which wound up as the B side of the 1976 single "TVC 15."

"TVC 15" was the second release from *Station to Station,* an ambitious R&B-inflected album that had already spawned the sparkling hit "Golden Years." The six-song *Station* continued Bowie's fruitful association with guitarist Carlos Alomar (co-writer, with Bowie and John Lennon, of "Fame"), and for the accompanying tour Bowie added to his long list of stage personae the character of "the Thin White Duke." The icy Duke was a far cry from previous incarnations like Ziggy Stardust and Aladdin Sane, but—typical of Bowie—it was right for the disco-cool moment. From the hypnotic chug of the ten-minute title track to the smooth funk of "Stay," *Station to Station* proved a worthy successor to 1975's *Young Americans,* and Bowie now considers it among his best work. The year 1976—in many ways Bowie's biggest—also included a platinum greatest-hits package (*ChangesOneBowie*), a *Rolling Stone* cover, and a starring role in Nicolas Roeg's underrated *The Man Who Fell to Earth* (the film that put the "alien" in "alienation"); even Bowie's former backup band, the Spiders from Mars, released an album. The artist was not yet thirty.

Before undertaking another album project, Bowie left his adopted home of Los Angeles for the humbler environs of working-class West Berlin. As mentioned, he took Iggy Pop with him, but more importantly, he began a three-album collaboration with studio wunderkind and former Roxy Music synthesist Brian Eno. The "Eno Trilogy"—as *Low, Heroes,* and *Lodger* are known collectively—was extraordinarily influential, laying the groundwork for everyone from Gary Numan and Ultravox to Simple Minds and the Psychedelic Furs. *Low,* in particular, created numerous new non-mainstream Bowie fans, and the half-vocal, half-instrumental LP has become the *Sgt. Pepper* of ambient rock. Its rough edges and short, explosive songs are the main reason Bowie escaped the scorn punk rockers so generously heaped on his long-winded contemporaries.

West Germany was also home to techno-rockers like Kraftwerk and Tangerine Dream, not to mention ponderous "progressive" bands like Triumvirat and Nektar, and *Low* showed signs of these influences, too. Filtered through Eno's distorting lens, though, the squeaky-clean sonic vistas of Kraftwerk's *Autobahn* became sooty, sweaty, dystopic *Blade Runner*-style nightmares. Bowie was such an accomplished rock songwriter that his core fans were initially frustrated to find him steering clear of his strengths, but the Eno Trilogy now seems a logical outgrowth of *Station to Station.* In the wake of the tuneless clatter of "alternative rock," trifles like "Sound and Vision" (1977) sound positively Gershwinesque. For a good souvenir of the period, Bowie's second double live album, *Stage* (1978) is recommended.

Pete Townshend has said that "the decline of the Roman Empire is what happened in the seventies." If that's true—and given the decade's hedonistic opulence (and the marked increase in public bathing), it probably is—there was none better than David Bowie to navigate the downslope. His music reeked of decadence—even, at times, exalted in it, and songs like "Heroes" and "Golden Years" ("Run for the shadows . . .") represented credible responses to the dying of the light. During his "Berlin period," he allowed elegance and trashiness to coexist as no rocker ever had; other than Bryan Ferry, no other rocker had ever really tried. *Station to Station* is as timeless as the work of a master of transience can be.

Bowie's own artistic decline would follow swiftly. *Scary Monsters* (1980) was a credible coda to his seventies work, but by the time of his stint as a coiffed, multiplatinum video dandy in the mid-1980s, he seemed to have finally exhausted his reservoir of unfailing artistry. The fact that *Let's Dance* brought him unprecedented financial success means nothing; the public often catches up with an innovator just in time to miss everything that made him or her important (see also, Kate Bush). If the smirky dance-floor bluster of *Let's Dance* was perfect for the Reagan-Thatcher era, it was to the detriment of the music: "Modern Love" doesn't stand up to "Changes" any more than "Silly Love Songs" stands up to "Penny Lane," and there was nothing serious about the Serious Moonlight Tour. Fortunately for Bowie, the modern audience seems to understand that his mid-seventies masterworks—everything from *Hunky Dory* to *Low*—are what make him worthy of all the fuss.

Wavelengths

SINGER-SONGWRITERS

"Still Crazy After All These Years" • Paul Simon (Columbia, 1976)
"In France They Kiss on Main Street" • Joni Mitchell (Asylum, 1976)
"Baltimore" • Randy Newman (Warner Bros., 1977)
"Burma Shave" • Tom Waits (Elektra, 1977)
"Running On Empty" • Jackson Browne (Asylum, 1978)
"Boys in the Trees" • Carly Simon (Elektra, 1978)
"Love and Affection" • Joan Armatrading (A&M, 1978)
"Excitable Boy" • Warren Zevon (Elektra, 1978)
"Gotta Serve Somebody" • Bob Dylan (Columbia, 1979)
"My My, Hey Hey (Out of the Blue)" • Neil Young & Crazy Horse (Reprise, 1979)

As Jimmy Page has observed, the word "genius" comes up an awful lot in rock and roll, and nowhere has this been truer than in the realm of the singer-songwriter. Free from the glitzier requirements of rock stardom, and often saddled with the weighty adjunct "poet," singer-songwriters have been variously hailed as prophets, revolutionaries, and chroniclers of their times. Songs like "The Sounds of Silence," "You Can't Always Get What You Want," "Like a Rolling Stone," "Imagine," "Heart of Gold," and "Both Sides Now," are among the most lauded of the rock era, and are widely held as works of genius.

In many respects, the songwriting climate of the late seventies was much like today's. Then, as now, any even slightly above-average Bob Dylan album had critics doing handstands. Early albums by Joni Mitchell, Neil Young, and James

Taylor were touchstones. And new voices were emerging constantly, often to hyperbolic praise. (One key difference: Back then, most of the "geniuses" were men.)

Into this fertile environment spilled some of the best work of Bruce Springsteen, Elvis Costello, Bob Marley, James Taylor, Rickie Lee Jones, Steely Dan, David Bowie, Billy Joel, and the Eagles (all covered separately in this book). In addition, many core voices endured. For Joni Mitchell, whose biggest commercial success (1974's *Court and Spark*) was already behind her, the late seventies were a period of experimentation. *Hejira* (1976), arguably the best album of her career, employed a scaled-down band that included the late Weather Report bassist Jaco Pastorius and session guitar god Larry Carlton. Songs like "Coyote" (a frenetic rap to a freewheeling cowboy lover), "Song for Sharon" (a sprawling meditation on

CROSBY, STILLS & NASH
Tonight 8 p.m.
maple leaf gardens
tickets $8.50 & 9.50
Available at the door

love, family, and the life of the outsider), and the title track (perhaps the best song ever written about transience) found Mitchell's already unparalleled lyrical skills sharpened to a laser-fine point. If you were willing to follow her muse through sonorous images like "White flags of winter chimneys / Wave truce against the moon," the rewards were considerable, and not all verbal/intellectual; the then common allegation that the artist had forsaken her melodic gifts seems, in hindsight, absurd.

Mitchell's other late-seventies albums, the double-LP, part-orchestral excursion *Don Juan's Reckless Daughter,* and *Mingus,* her collaboration with jazz bassist and composer Charles Mingus (who was then dying of Amyotrophic Lateral Sclerosis), met with mixed reviews, although both did well on the charts. Answering her critics, Mitchell said, "I crave change and I assumed that I was in sync with my times and other people needing change would be able to follow." Over-estimating your audience is one of the foibles of being a genius (there's that word again).

Longtime Mitchell friend and rival Bob Dylan released five albums between 1976 and 1979, including the Rolling Thunder Revue live set *Hard Rain,* the chart-topping *Desire,* and the born-again *Slow Train Coming* (featuring guest Mark Knopfler on "Gotta Serve Somebody"). Van Morrison, who also found religion in the last days of the seventies, notched a minor hit in 1978 with his tribute to radio, "Wavelength." Neil Young straddled folk (*Comes a Time*) and hard rock (*Rust Never Sleeps*), winning critics' polls and new fans alike.

After releasing four albums in four years and taking top honors at the 1975 Grammy Awards for *Still Crazy After All These Years,* Paul Simon slowed his solo recording pace considerably, contributing only one new song (the elegant "Slip Sliding Away") to his best-selling 1977 career retrospective

Greatest Hits, Etc. Meanwhile, he collaborated with Art Garfunkel and James Taylor on "(What a) Wonderful World"; made a TV special; appeared on *Saturday Night Live;* acted the part of a smarmy record producer in Woody Allen's *Annie Hall;* and began work on *One Trick Pony,* the semi-autobiographical movie that would ultimately drag its excellent soundtrack down with it after a limited release in 1980.

West Coast irony specialist, and sometime Simon collaborator, Randy Newman found his commercial touch—maybe by accident—with 1977's *Little Criminals.* Infamous for the misunderstood novelty hit "Short People," the album also contained some of Newman's best work, notably the stark urban portrait "Baltimore." Warren Zevon, also the beneficiary of a novelty hit ("Werewolves of London"), made the exceptional *Excitable Boy* in 1978 with his friend Jackson Browne. Browne's own "Running On Empty"—an irresistibly catchy salute to the spiritually bankrupt, self-obsessed seventies—eventually became one of the era's signature songs.

Implicit in "Running On Empty" (and contemporaneous songs like Newman's "It's Money That I Love") was the death of sixties idealism, and, to be sure, the American political climate had changed considerably since the heady days of the protest movement and the Vietnam War: Jerry Falwell observed correctly, if self-servingly, that America was "fed up with radical causes"; Harvard University ditched the looser curricula it had adopted in the early 1970s; LSD champion Timothy Leary lamented the mainstreaming of illicit drugs; and Ronald Reagan began the dubious tradition (now firmly entrenched in the electoral process) of using "liberal" as a pejorative term.

Many singer-songwriters responded to the political big chill by focusing their energies inward (Mitchell, Taylor, Bruce

Cockburn). Others penned third-person stories full of ironic perspective (Newman, Zevon, Graham Parker). Still others, mostly those connected with punk and other emerging styles, raged against the dying of the good fight with socially conscious, sometimes angry music (Costello, Marley, Tom Petty).

Tom Waits, for his part, was unclassifiable. Weaving vivid stories of the down-and-out post-beatnik types with whom he associated, sometimes using layers of imagery in place of narrative line, he carved out a niche that he alone was able to occupy (though Rickie Lee Jones spent some time there—that's her on the back cover of 1978's *Blue Valentine*). "Burma Shave," from 1977's *Foreign Affairs,* was emblematic of the period. From the drifter and small-town girl who hook up for a crime spree, to the brilliant conceit of naming the small town in question after a long-lost, all-American product, the song's sketchy plot is illustrated in lines so perfectly wrought that even if Waits had composed nothing else that year, "Burma Shave" would have sufficed. The America-in-the-thirties theme is central, too: Waits always seemed to be marooned in the wrong decade. Waits would create an even more rarefied space for himself with his mid-1980s trilogy (*Swordfishtrombones, Rain Dogs,* and *Franks Wild Years*), singing in several different voices as he inhabited his poignant, damaged characters.

Also wont to sing in multiple voices was the prolific prog-rock diva Kate Bush, whose gorgeous debut single "Wuthering Heights" (1978) went to number one in England. Descended more from the Peter Gabriel/Pink Floyd school than the troubadour tradition—it was Floyd guitarist David Gilmour who originally brought her to the attention of EMI—Bush made great records but only slight inroads into the U.S. market during the seventies. "The Man with the Child in His

Eyes" (number 85, 1979) was her lone *Billboard*-charting single of the decade. Her followers were legion, however, and her influence on the current arty crop of female writers (Tori Amos, Paula Cole, et al.) is incalculable.

The singer-songwriter field was so crowded in the late seventies that entire careers were unfolding outside the hit parade. Significant '76–'79 non-charters included Laura Nyro, Richard Thompson, Loudon Wainwright III, Leonard Cohen, John Prine, Janis Ian, Gil Scott-Heron, Steve Goodman, David Bromberg, Garland Jeffreys, Elliott Murphy, John Hiatt, Lou Reed, Joan Armatrading, Lowell George (Little Feat), and Andy Partridge (XTC). It may seem contradictory that the art of songwriting flourished during the age of the blockbuster—a culture hungry for ABBA and the Bee Gees would not, at first glance, seem ripe for the thoughtful types described above—but similar mysteries existed in all the written arts: What had Sam Shepard to do with Neil Simon, or Kurt Vonnegut Jr. with Arthur Hailey? It may have been, as Lowell George commented shortly before his death in 1979, simply that "the music business generates around good songs." It did then, anyway.

THY THEE THINE: Songwriters Look Beyond the Self

If you think the 1970s' singer-songwriters were a navel-gazing bunch unconnected to the world around them, check out these cause-and-effect relationships:

- A large ore vessel sinks in Lake Erie in the fall of 1975: Gordon Lightfoot commemorates the event in "The Wreck of the Edmund Fitzgerald."
- Boxer Rubin "Hurricane" Carter is convicted of murder: Bob Dylan writes "Hurricane" to raise public awareness of the case.

- Prominent British fascist Oswald Mosley experiences a resurgence in popularity: Elvis Costello responds angrily with "Less Than Zero."
- The Three Mile Island accident and the Karen Silkwood case cause widespread fear of nuclear power: Bonnie Raitt, Jackson Browne and others found MUSE (Musicians United for Safe Energy).
- The Cold War escalates and détente is strained as bugging devices are discovered in the U.S. embassy in Moscow: Talking Heads give voice to the gathering storm in "Life During Wartime."
- The U.S. celebrates its bicentennial in 1976: With "Black Man," Stevie Wonder reminds his countrymen that the past two hundred years have not been without shame.
- The Sex Pistols cause outrage in England by, among other things, slamming Elizabeth II in "God Save the Queen": Neil Young responds with "My My, Hey Hey (Out of the Blue)," an ode to Pistols frontman Johnny Rotten.
- Jimmy Carter grants Vietnam draft dodgers unconditional amnesty: Jesse Winchester returns from Canada, resumes U.S. career.
- World terrorism and professionally fought wars are on the rise: Warren Zevon writes the darkly hilarious "Roland the Headless Thompson Gunner" about an international gun-for-hire.
- Violence erupts frequently in racially charged, economically stratified Los Angeles: Steely Dan's Walter Becker and Donald Fagen pen "Don't Take Me Alive," an L.A.-inspired story of a standoff between police and an armed "bookkeeper's son."

Carly's Angel

JAMES TAYLOR

"Shower the People" • James Taylor (Warner Bros., 1976)
"Handy Man" • James Taylor (Columbia, 1977)
"Your Smiling Face" • James Taylor (Columbia, 1977)
"Secret o' Life" • James Taylor (Columbia, 1977)
"Honey Don't Leave L.A." • James Taylor (Columbia, 1978)
"(What a) Wonderful World" • Art Garfunkel with James Taylor and Paul Simon
(Columbia, 1978)
"Devoted to You" • Carly Simon and James Taylor (Elektra, 1978)
"You Belong to Me" • Carly Simon (Elektra, 1978)
"I Will Be In Love with You" • Livingston Taylor (Epic, 1978)
"Up On the Roof" • James Taylor (Columbia, 1979)

The life which is unexamined is not worth living.

—Plato

They called him "Mr. Sensitive." The "troubled troubadour." They said he did for introspection what *The Ami-
tyville Horror* did for real-estate values in upstate New York.
They derided him for betraying the very function of art (to
hold a mirror up to life), alleging he would rather hold the
looking glass up . . . to himself. One of them even fantasized
about mutilating him with a broken bottle.

They are the critics, and he is James Taylor, one of a handful of rock-era songwriters who can claim to have contributed
significantly to the Great American Songbook. In the early
seventies, when he became the quintessential male folkie

(Joni was the female), Taylor was one of the few coffeehouse types writing anything resembling a standard. A sort of back-woods Bacharach, he easily navigated the narrow peninsula that separates the Gulf of Gershwin from Dylan Bay; unlike the previous generation of professional songsmiths, who had custom-tailored their work for theatrical characters, he wrote first-person monologues for himself to sing.

From the beginning, the critics were hostile. Then as now, they preferred sheer volume to volubility, and an acoustic artiste of James's ilk was in constant danger of being thrown off the Jefferson Airplane with no parachute. Crafty, inter-nally rhyming lyrics, fluid storytelling, and harmonic sophisti-cation were beside the point. Taylor just plain talked (sang) about himself too much. The fact that his navel-gazing days were all but over by the time of his great 1977 album *J.T.* was irrelevant: he had been painted with the "narcissist" brush, and that's some goddamned durable paint.

By the mid-seventies, the artist had been institutionalized twice—once for heroin addiction, once for severe depres-sion—and had more to get off his chest, perhaps, than the next guy. Still, he broke up traditional J.T. fare like "Shower the People" (about the healing power of love) and "Secret o' Life" (about living in the moment) with character studies like "Brother Trucker" and "Millworker," songs at least as far from his experience as "George Jackson" was from Bob Dylan's. In the self-obsessed Carter years, then, "Mr. Sensitive" began to become noticeably less self-obsessed.

The period was a hot one for Taylor, despite paternal re-sponsibilities and the vigilance required to keep his demons at bay. He was all over the radio, with covers of Jimmy Jones's "Handy Man," the Drifters' "Up On the Roof," and Sam Cooke's "Wonderful World" (with Simon and Garfunkel) hit-ting big, and his own ebullient "Your Smiling Face" going Top

Twenty. *Greatest Hits* commemorated his years with Warner Brothers, eventually selling into the tens of millions. And his presence was felt at the New York "No Nukes" benefit and on wife Carly Simon's uncharacteristically superb *Boys in the Trees*.

In The Pocket (1976) featured at least two should-have-been hits ("Junkie's Lament" and the Stevie Wonder collaboration "Don't Be Sad 'Cause Your Sun Is Down"), but underperformed by the standards of its follow-up, released the next summer. *J.T.*, Taylor's first taste of platinum, was wall-to-wall excellence, mixing chunky, soulful rock ("Honey Don't Leave L.A.") and broad comedy ("Traffic Jam") with subtler material like "Another Grey Morning." The acronym made good marketing sense, too; James Taylor was by then a dependable brand name.

Or was he? *Flag* (1979), featuring a photograph of the thin, tired-looking artist on its inner sleeve, and an unintentional rendering of the nautical symbol for "man overboard" on its cover, was higher in filler than its predecessor. From an ill-advised take on the Beatles' "Day Tripper" (song overboard) to the Berlitz-pop of "Chanson Française," the somewhat downbeat set surrounded diamonds like "B.S.U.R." and "Rainy Day Man" with a little too much rough.

At decade's end, J.T. was struggling with writer's block and a waning marriage. Carly told *Rolling Stone* in 1981 that her husband was "most healthy" when he was on tour, and, within two years, they were divorced. Since then, Taylor has toured virtually nonstop, drawing diehard fans who'll "pay good money to hear 'Fire and Rain' again and again and again," and releasing personal—but not too personal—albums like *Never Die Young* (1988) and *Hourglass* (1998) along the way.

Coolsville

RICKIE LEE JONES

"Blue Valentines" • Tom Waits (Elektra, 1978)
"Easy Money" • Lowell George (Warner Bros., 1979)
"Chuck E.'s in Love" • Rickie Lee Jones (Warner Bros., 1979)
"Young Blood" • Rickie Lee Jones (Warner Bros., 1979)
"On Saturday Afternoons in 1963" • Rickie Lee Jones (Warner Bros., 1979)
"Company" • Rickie Lee Jones (Warner Bros., 1979)
"Easy Money" • Rickie Lee Jones (Warner Bros., 1979)
"The Last Chance Texaco" • Rickie Lee Jones (Warner Bros., 1979)
"Night Train" • Rickie Lee Jones (Warner Bros., 1979)
"Danny's All-Star Joint" • Rickie Lee Jones (Warner Bros., 1979)

When pop star Melissa Manchester opined in 1979 that "there are still a lot of feminine points of view that haven't been expressed musically yet," she didn't know the half of it. The years ahead would see landmark records by female artists as disparate as Laurie Anderson, Suzanne Vega, Tracy Chapman, Sinéad O'Connor, Queen Latifah, Alanis Morissette, and Lauryn Hill and, in the short term, the stunning debut of one of the seventies' most original voices, Rickie Lee Jones.

A Chicago-born teenage runaway who drifted into Venice, California, in the late seventies, Jones began her career performing free for "bikers, degenerates, drunken men and toothless women" (her description). The daughter of a songwriter—she recorded her father's "The Moon Is Made of Gold" on the 1988 Rob Wasserman album *Duets*—she soon began composing her own songs, many of them jazzy monologues along the lines of Tom Waits's "Diamonds On My Windshield." One of these, "Easy Money," was recorded by ex–Little Feat big cheese Lowell George (*Thanks I'll Eat It Here*, 1979), and, within the year, Warner's Russ Titleman and Lenny Waronker had produced the twenty-four-year-old Jones's eponymous debut using a who's who of L.A. session players.

Positive reaction to the album's breezy, lightly swinging leadoff single, "Chuck E.'s In Love," was immediate. The song climbed to number 4 on *Billboard*'s Hot 100, spurring *Rickie Lee Jones* to platinum sales and a number 3 berth on the album chart. Meanwhile, Jones's jazzy image and against-the-current attitude generated lots of press, including a *Time* magazine profile and a *Rolling Stone* cover story. Her new peers in the National Academy of Recording Arts and Sciences rewarded her with a Best New Artist Grammy in 1979. And Chuck E. Weiss, a real-life mutual friend of Jones and Waits, became a SoCal celebrity. In the end, the frenzy of attention established a commercial standard the adventurous Jones would never again approach.

Lost in the rapturous praise for "Chuck E.'s In Love" and the similarly funky follow-up single "Youngblood," were Jones's deeper attributes as a songwriter: her post-Kerouac literary spirit ("Coolsville," "Last Chance Texaco"), her dead-accurate, street-level humor ("Danny's All-Star Joint," "Weasel and the White Boys Cool"), and, most of all, her virtually unprecedented, soul-baring tenderness ("Company," "Night Train," "On Saturday Afternoons in 1963"). The settings were full of airy, open chord voicings, references to 1950s musical theater, huge dynamics (barrelhouse louds and whispering softs), and memorable instrumental flourishes—Steve Gadd's four-over-three break on "Chuck E.'s In Love" was the drum fill of the decade. Jones sang in a rhythmically free, expressive slur, treating her own compositions the way jazz musicians treat standards.

The emotional scope and poetic bent of the music on *Rickie Lee Jones* inevitably led to comparisons with Joni Mitchell. Jones bristled, saying she owed far more to Van Morrison (she wasn't kidding; "Chuck E." 's signature guitar line is a direct descendant of "Domino," and the influence of Morrison's *Astral Weeks* got even more pronounced on Jones's *Pirates* [1981]), but Mitchell's work was paradigmatic—unavoidable—in those days. There could no more have been Rickie Lee Jones without Joni Mitchell than there could be Sheryl Crow without Rickie Lee Jones.

Even in 1979, a year dominated by West Coast blockbusters like the Eagles' *The Long Run* and the Doobie Brothers' *Minute by Minute,* Jones outcooled, outfunnied, outsang, outcomposed, and generally outdid her L.A. brethren. Her influence was not immediately apparent in the ten years following (with the flagrant exception of Edie Brickell), but many current artists owe her a great debt. And if she can't take credit for "elbow[ing] all the disco aside," as *Time* predicted she would—disco was already on life support by late 1979—she certainly raised the stakes of the singer-songwriter game, creating expectations even she sometimes has trouble meeting.

The Girls in the Plastic Bubbles

DIVAS

"That'll Be the Day" • Linda Ronstadt (Asylum, 1976)
"My Heart Belongs to Me" • Barbra Streisand (Columbia, 1977)
"Nobody Does It Better" • Carly Simon (Elektra, 1977)
"Right Time of the Night" • Jennifer Warnes (Arista, 1977)
"I've Got Love On My Mind" • Natalie Cole (Capitol, 1977)
"We're All Alone" • Rita Coolidge (A&M, 1977)
"You Needed Me" • Anne Murray (Capitol, 1978)
"Lotta Love" • Nicolette Larson (Warner Bros., 1978)
"Don't Cry Out Loud" • Melissa Manchester (Arista, 1978)
"I'll Never Love This Way Again" • Dionne Warwick (Arista, 1979)

Snapshots of the women's movement, 1976–79: Women enter NASA's astronaut training program. Over 100,000 women march on Washington, D.C., in support of the Equal Rights Amendment. For the first time, a woman is awarded a Rhodes scholarship. The federal reserve mints the Susan B. Anthony dollar. Margaret Thatcher is elected prime minister of Britain. An all-female crew "mans" a train from Washington, New York, to New York City. A woman commands a U.S. Navy ship. A Muhammad Ali fight is refereed by a woman. Bella Abzug lobbies for equal pay for equal work. Movies like *An Unmarried Woman* give the female perspective on divorce.

And big-time female vocalists respond—with total disinterest. Though cutting-edge artists like Joni Mitchell, Rickie Lee Jones, and Kate Bush were broadening horizons with every syllable they sang, the diva contingent seemed content either to warble corporate ballads or to reinterpret time-tested chestnuts from the rock era.

Hiring a bona fide singer-songwriter to cut the new James Bond song might have seemed like progress back in 1977, but "Nobody Does It Better," Carly Simon's theme to *The Spy Who Loved Me,* was as traditional and showy as "Goldfinger." For those already familiar with the Alan Parsons Project's "Don't Let It Show," Melissa Manchester's "Don't Cry Out Loud" was old news, and, in extreme cases, resulted in pleas of, "Don't *sing* out loud." Dionne Warwick's shrill "I'll Never Love This Way Again" was to her sixties-era Bacharach-David sides what Bo Derek was to Ann-Margret. And Barbra Streisand, even then queen of the divas, was maintaining her lifestyle with songs like "My Heart Belongs to Me" while interpreting more worthy contemporary material (Billy Joel's "New York State of Mind," Kenny Loggins's "I Believe in Love") on the sly.

Linda Ronstadt, just homey enough (the cowboy boots, the eyelet blouses) and just sexy enough (the roller skates, the silk shorts) to appeal to every possible demographic, was the best-selling solo voice of her day. She belted, she crooned, she even rocked. And though her albums occasionally seemed overly market-ready, she had good taste in covers: from classic rock and soul (Chuck Berry's "Back in the U.S.A.," the Miracles' "Tracks of My Tears" and "Ooo Baby Baby," Buddy Holly's "That'll Be the Day" and "It's So Easy") to contemporary, A-list songwriting (Warren Zevon's "Poor Poor Pitiful Me," Jagger and Richards's "Tumbling Dice," Elvis Costello's "Alison" and "Girls Talk"), Ronstadt's repertoire was almost always above average.

The same was true of Phoebe Snow, the New York R&B expert known for the gentle ballad "Poetry Man." She had a minor hit in 1977 with the Temptations' "Shakey Ground," also covering Stephen Bishop's "Never Letting Go" and Paul Simon's "Something So Right." Bette Midler balanced Bobby Freeman's "Do You Want to Dance" (1958) with James Taylor's "Millworker," Billy Joel's "Say Goodbye to Hollywood," and Tom Waits's "I Never Talk to Strangers." Nicolette Larson, the "Rhumba Girl," brought Neil Young's "Lotta Love" out of album-cut oblivion.

In cases where the artist wasn't hunting down fresh material, however, the cover phenomenon smacked of opportunism. *Q:* Were any of the following '76–'79 versions definitive?

- Melba Moore—"Lean On Me"
- Bonnie Raitt—"Runaway"
- Bonnie Tyler—"Natural Woman"

Hair-port '77: the "Farrah"

- Barbra Streisand—"Splish Splash"
- Anne Murray—"Daydream Believer"
- Jennifer Warnes—"Don't Make Me Over"
- Crystal Gayle—"Cry Me a River"
- Melissa Manchester; Linda Ronstadt—"Rescue Me"
- Rita Coolidge; Dolly Parton—"Higher and Higher"

Sometimes a diva in search of fresh material would choose unwelcome hits of the day that had only just disappeared. How else to explain Dionne Warwick's day-old covers of Olivia Newton-John's "Have You Never Been Mellow" and The Captain and Tennille's "The Way I Want to Touch You"?

When all else failed, Beatles covers were a good option. Phoebe Snow's "In My Life," Melba Moore's "The Long and Winding Road," Emmylou Harris's "Here, There and Everywhere," Natalie Cole's "Lucy in the Sky with Diamonds," and Anne Murray's "Day Tripper" stayed well clear of the Top 40, but at least their source was unimpeachable.

Compared to the post-grunge singer-songwriter renaissance of the mid-1990s (a fast-evolving, popularly supported movement led almost entirely by women), the female pop scene of the late seventies seems almost inert. "Shadows in the Moonlight." "Blue Bayou." "Don't It Make My Brown Eyes Blue." The divas were in the doldrums, and they would have done well to heed this 1977 advice from Joan Armatrading, their West Indian compatriot: "Show some emotion!"

Platinum Bland

MOR

"There's a Kind of Hush (All Over the World)" • Carpenters (A&M, 1976)
"After the Lovin'" • Engelbert Humperdinck (Epic, 1976)
"Lost Without Your Love" • Bread (Elektra, 1976)
"You Light Up My Life" • Debby Boone (Warner Bros., 1977)
"When I Need You" • Leo Sayer (Warner Bros., 1977)
"Looks Like We Made It" • Barry Manilow (Arista, 1977)
"Say You'll Stay Until Tomorrow" • Tom Jones (Epic, 1977)
"Way Down" • Elvis Presley (RCA, 1977)
"You Don't Bring Me Flowers" • Barbra Streisand and Neil Diamond (Columbia, 1978)
"Do That to Me One More Time" • The Captain & Tennille (Casablanca, 1979)

In 1976, Jimmy Carter's misery index—the sum of America's unemployment and inflation rates—was 12.4. For a more accurate measure of suffering in the U.S., Carter might have factored in the number of current Barry Manilow singles (which would have brought the misery index to 16.4); the number of Neil Sedaka songs covered by Wayne Newton ("The Hungry Years"—13.4); or even the number of records sold by the Captain & Tennille since their 1975 debut (20,000,012.4).

In any event, one number couldn't begin to describe life in the mush age. Once again proving itself to be the world's most evergreen musical style, middle-of-the-road (MOR) weathered the disco and punk threats, consistently outperforming its often worthy competition: Debby Boone's maudlin "You Light Up My Life" stayed at number one for ten weeks, as brilliant singles by Steely Dan, James Taylor, and Boz Scaggs missed the Top Ten entirely. Tom Jones went country ("Say You'll Stay Until Tomorrow"), Andy Williams went soul ("Tell It Like It Is"), the Carpenters went retro ("There's a Kind of Hush"). Most telling of all, Bread reformed.

Amid suspicious reports of government-sanctioned mind-control experiments, the most boring cocktail party in the galaxy continued, with "lite" favorites old (Kenny Rogers, Bobby Vinton) and new (Leo Sayer, Andy Gibb) notching Hot 100 hits. Love was in the air. Love was thicker than water. Love was a boat, one it would take some kind of cataclysmic event to rock.

That event arrived on August 16, 1977, when rock-and-roll singer, B-movie star, religious icon, secret-agent wannabe, Beatles hater, jumpsuit wearer, and Las Vegas regular Elvis Presley died at his Memphis home (known as Graceland, now one of the South's biggest tourist attractions). By then, his current work was of little concern to the general public—

"Way Down" (1977) proved to be aptly titled—but Elvis's legend still loomed large, especially to the aging MOR fans who remembered dodging stick shifts to "Love Me Tender." In the wake of Presley's death, tributes like Merle Haggard's "From Graceland to the Promised Land" appeared, RCA's catalog sales surged, and the world of soft rock mourned its King, though for all the wrong reasons; to this day, mutton-chopped impersonators and bogus sightings blur the legacy of Presley's great fifties recordings.

Way down, but not out, second-generation Elvis devotees like Neil Diamond and Engelbert Humperdinck continued their mission: the oversweetening of pop. The greeting-card agenda seldom changed, whether the current record was a platinum duet with Barbra Streisand ("You Don't Bring Me Flowers") or a postcoital serenade ("After the Lovin'"). MOR was a genre in which "Torn Between Two Lovers" constituted high drama. It was the suede elbow patch on the sport coat called rock and roll.

Questions lingered. Was *Barry Manilow—Live* an oxymoron? How could Anita Bryant in good conscience endorse oranges while attacking "fruits"? If erasable ink was on the market as early as 1978, why couldn't it have been used for the lyrics to "Escape (The Piña Colada Song)"? And if "Do That to Me One More Time" was so sexy, why did "Muskrat Love" sound hot by comparison?

No answer was forthcoming; MOR simply went on, like a force of nature, unexplained—maybe unexplainable. It continued to be a commercial staple throughout the eighties and early nineties, launching gross-national-product–size careers like those of Lionel Richie, Mariah Carey, and Boyz II Men (make no mistake, all of the above are MOR, even if the term "adult contemporary" now applies). It is the engine that drives the film-soundtrack business, the spokesmusic for bro-kenhearted lovers everywhere. And still its biggest stars head inexorably west to Vegas, like a caravan of well-heeled buskers dragging their possessions (Grammys, Oscars, gold bullion) behind them in a surreal, made-for-TV *Grapes of Wrath.*

The Wonder Years

SOUL

"I Wish" • Stevie Wonder (Tamla, 1976)
"Something He Can Feel" • Aretha Franklin (Atlantic, 1976)
"Disco Lady" • Johnnie Taylor (Columbia, 1976)
"Kiss and Say Goodbye" • The Manhattans (Columbia, 1976)
"Misty Blue" • Dorothy Moore (Malaco, 1976)
"Got to Give It Up (Part I)" • Marvin Gaye (Tamla, 1977)
"Use Ta Be My Girl" • O'Jays (Philadelphia International, 1978)
"Crusin'" • Smokey Robinson (Tamla, 1979)
"Soul Man" • Blues Brothers (Atlantic, 1979)
"Working My Way Back to You" • Spinners (Atlantic, 1979)

There had been arguments about the death of rock and roll at least as far back as Elvis Presley's 1958 stint in the army, but the decline of black popular music had been largely ignored until Nelson George's 1991 book *The Death of Rhythm and Blues* described the industry's long, slow war against soul. George offered a dispiriting account of the small battles and compromises that had chipped away at the music over the years, and located the actual "death" sometime in the late seventies.

The years 1976–79 were a time of confusion in the R&B world. Despite the gains of the previous twenty years, it seemed fewer and fewer artists were pursuing their chosen directions unburdened by financial pressure. Johnnie Taylor, a veteran soul man whose contract was acquired from Stax by

Columbia in 1976, saw the writing on the wall when the languid, bandwagon-jumping single "Disco Lady" became his biggest hit ever. Isaac Hayes, past his *Shaft*-era prime, cast about for a hit, climbing to number 18 with 1979's "Don't Let Go" before disappearing quietly from the pop charts. Aretha Franklin, still the Queen of Soul but fast losing her mainstream audience, brought in *Superfly* producer Curtis Mayfield in 1976, but to no avail. Al Green had taken to the pulpit. Gladys Knight was out of gas. The Temptations were treading water.

Moving with the times involved pragmatism. Though many considered making disco records a fatal concession to popular tastes, the influence of the dance floor is hard to miss on Marvin Gaye's "Got to Give It Up (Pt. 1)" (number one, 1977) and the O'Jays' "Use Ta Be My Girl" (number 4, 1978). Bona fide stand-alone soul hits like Dorothy Moore's "Misty Blue" and the Manhattans' "Kiss and Say Goodbye" were all but extinct.

Then, a ray of hope. Word escaped from Los Angeles that Stevie Wonder was preparing to break his two-year silence: He had signed a new, record-setting contract with Motown and was mixing a two-record opus that would advance the legacy of *Talking Book, Innervisions,* and *Fulfillingness' First Finale.*

Songs in the Key of Life, as it turned out, was two records and then some, for it included a bonus four-song EP (Stevie had so much material this time around that four sides weren't enough). Including four hits—"I Wish," "Sir Duke," "Another Star," and "As"—the album was immediately embraced by a public hungry for a fresh R&B/pop synthesis. Nonstop brilliant, and peppered with ambitious excursions like the fusion-tinged "Contusion," the pseudo-classical "Village Ghetto Land," and the harp-and-voice "If It's Magic," *Songs* was almost overwhelming in its sheer melodic density. After multiple listenings, though, individual tracks began to distinguish themselves, and fans giddily realized they were in the presence of that rare LP that was without a weak moment (some griped about the longish songs, but the grooves were so fierce you could forgive Stevie for wanting to stretch out a little on the fades).

Songs would garner four Grammys, stay atop the *Billboard* album chart for over three months, and put its author in a position of extraordinary power. The followup, *Journey Into the Secret Life of Plants* (1979), would diminish that power somewhat, however: its lone hit, "Send One Your Love," was not enough for Stevie's now rabid followers. If R&B was in even worse shape than before—Johnnie Taylor had now put his name to "Disco 9000"—it certainly was not Stevie Wonder's doing. *Songs in the Key of Life* showed the world how it should be done, and perhaps its so-so sequel showed the world that Stevie couldn't do it alone. Most important, *Songs* helped a disco-saturated world believe, if only temporarily, that reports of the death of soul had been greatly exaggerated.

Movin' On Up

CORPORATE SOUL

"This Masquerade" • George Benson (Warner Brothers, 1976)

"You'll Never Find Another Love Like Mine" • Lou Rawls (Philadelphia International, 1976)

"Themes from *Mahogany* (Do You Know Where You're Going To)" • Diana Ross (Motown, 1976)

"You Don't Have to Be a Star (To Be in My Show)" • Marilyn McCoo & Billy Davis Jr. (ABC, 1976)

"Three Times a Lady" • Commodores (Motown, 1978)

"The Closer I Get to You" • Roberta Flack and Donny Hathaway (Atlantic, 1978)

"Too Much, Too Little, Too Late" • Johnny Mathis and Deniece Williams (Columbia, 1978)

"Reunited" • Peaches & Herb (Polydor, 1979)

"Found a Cure" • Ashford & Simpson (Warner Brothers, 1979)

"With You I'm Born Again" • Billy Preston and Syreeta (Motown, 1979)

How many times does R&B go into MOR? That was the question facing the droves of high-glass late-seventies soul artists who, like George and Louise Jefferson, moved on up to the East Side in search of better things. The records that answered the question kept alive some worthy careers (Lou Rawls, Bill Withers), but often sounded like someone had put all the black music of the rock era into one of those then newfangled food processors and hit PUREE—"Reunited" and "Easy" still tasted like soul, but they were suspiciously smooth.

The rise of corporate soul coincided with the emergence of a bona fide black American middle class. From the ashes of the civil-rights movement had come a multitude of upwardly mobile black families, sequestered in many of the same suburbs from which they had once been barred, trying to make sense of life in mortgageland. The lifestyle of these proto-Huxtables was not necessarily reflected in the from-the-gut Southern soul of Otis Redding and Wilson Pickett or the inner-city funk of James Brown and George Clinton. A post-soul kind of easy listening was required, and "urban radio" was born.

At the center of the new format were the treacly ballads of Lionel Richie's Commodores, the "lite-jazz" of George Benson, and scores of mellow love duets by musical couples real (Ashford and Simpson, Marilyn McCoo and Billy Davis Jr.) and manufactured (Roberta Flack and Donny Hathaway, Peabo Bryson and Natalie Cole). These were songs capable of "crossing over"—selling to whites as well as blacks—and many of them attained high pop and adult-contemporary (AC) chart positions in addition to their R&B success [see chart].

The Commodores' case is an interesting one. In mid-1977, the six-year Motown veterans found themselves at a fork in the road, with a blistering number 5 hit ("Brick House") representing their hard-funk past and a tranquil number 4 hit ("Easy") heralding the emergence of silky-voiced lead singer Lionel Richie. Let the record show they chose door number two: Over the next five years, the band became the world's busiest ballad factory. "Three Times a Lady," perhaps Richie's best-known song, was an ingratiating trifle, but "Sail On" and "Still" (1979) hit deep emotional chords despite their calculated pan-format appeal. The Commodores still had occasional funk hits, but their more aggressive material was now generally relegated to B sides; "Sail On," for instance, was backed with "Thumpin' Music." Richie finally went solo in 1982, after recording "Endless Love" with Diana Ross.

Duet-mania was in full swing by 1976, when former 5th Dimension cohorts Marilyn McCoo and Billy Davis Jr. staged a comeback with "You Don't Have to Be a Star (To Be in My Show)" and, ironically, wound up starring in their own variety show. Crossover patriarch Johnny Mathis and soul ingenue Deniece Williams struck gold with "Too Much, Too Little, Too Late," then followed it up with "You're All I Need to Get By," an Ashford and Simpson chestnut from Motown's golden era. Peaches and Herb weighed in with "Reunited," the ultimate "our song" for on-again, off-again couples. Other coed balladry was supplied by Peabo Bryson and Natalie Cole, Billy Preston and Syreeta, and Roberta Flack and Donny Hathaway, whose "The Closer I Get to You" was released less than a year before Hathaway, one of the decade's great voices, took his own life in New York City.

Hathaway, it was observed, sounded something like George Benson, and both of them sounded something like Stevie Wonder. Benson silenced skeptics with his state-of-the-art production, fluid guitar solos, and shrewd song selection, not to mention his four *Breezin'* Grammys and all-time record for jazz album sales. His *Breezin'* hits, and follow-ups like "On Broadway" and the goosebump-inducing "Gonna Love You More," were miles ahead of the competition in the burgeoning "contemporary jazz" category, so far ahead that most pop fans wouldn't have known who the competition was (see "Sax and Violins: Corporate Jazz").

The inroads made by blacks into the mainstream of American life in the late seventies saw *Roots* (1977) drawing the largest television audience of all time, the FBI publicly apologizing for surveillance of Martin Luther King, and blacks holding jobs as disparate as astronaut and Mormon priest. Most telling of all, the decade ended with *The Jeffersons* in the Nielsen Top 10; the sitcom's story of a black family playing by the rules and prospering in America was not only fraught with comic possibilities—it was also reassuring to both blacks and whites.

Ditto most of this music: Lou Rawls may have been a South Side of Chicago–born, gospel-trained, legit R&B singer with hits dating back to 1965, but let's face it, "You'll Never Find Another Love Like Mine" wouldn't have gone to number one on the adult-contemporary chart unless it sounded really good coming from the ceiling of an elevator. Corporate soul split the difference between the classic Stax and Atlantic sides of the sixties and the slick, by-the-numbers songcraft that was late-seventies radio's stock-in-trade.

If the resulting test-tube baby didn't represent rhythm and blue's most memorable incarnation, it was also far from its worst (flash-forward to 1988, and you'll find George Michael atop the R&B chart). Crossover, after all, was not a new concept—it had been the explicit creed of early Motown—and the uptown soul of records like "On Broadway," "Easy," and "Reunited" has proved surprisingly durable. That doesn't make Marilyn McCoo Gladys Knight, nor does it excuse "Three Times a Lady," but upward mobility is human nature, and the East Side beckons.

Crossoverkill: Top Corporate Soul Singles 1976–79

SONG	#1 Pop	#1 AC	#1 R&B	Grammy	Gold	Platinum	TOTAL
"Reunited"	✓		✓		✓	✓	4
"Too Much, Too Little, Too Late"	✓	✓	✓		✓		4
"You Don't Have to Be a Star"	✓		✓	✓	✓		4
"Three Times a Lady"	✓	✓	✓				3
"You'll Never Find..."		✓	✓		✓		3
"Still"	✓		✓				2
"Theme from *Mahogany*"	✓	✓					2
"The Closer I Get to You"			✓		✓		2

Sgt. Pepper's "How Can You Mend a Broken Heart" Club Band

BEE GEES

"You Should Be Dancing" • Bee Gees (RSO, 1976)
"How Deep Is Your Love" • Bee Gees (RSO, 1977)
"Stayin' Alive" • Bee Gees (RSO, 1977)
"Emotion" • Samantha Sang (Private Stock, 1977)
"Night Fever" • Bee Gees (RSO, 1978)
"More Than a Woman" • Tavares (Capitol, 1978)
"If I Can't Have You" • Yvonne Elliman (RSO, 1978)
"Shadow Dancing" • Andy Gibb (RSO, 1978)
"Too Much Heaven" • Bee Gees (RSO, 1978)
"Tragedy" • Bee Gees (RSO, 1979)

If you'd been stopped on the street in, say, 1973 and told that within the space of a few years, soul's then rich kaleidoscope would collapse into a monochromatic formula that would inspire millions to dipsy-doodle onto the planet's dance floors in an empty, hedonistic frenzy, you'd have chuckled sympathetically at your "end is near" prophet and strolled away.

If, however, as you rejoined the flow of pedestrian traffic, the mangy man had given chase, ranting that this new soul-derived strain would be called "disco" and that no one would escape it, you might have accelerated to a light jog, for the first time slightly afraid. If, next, he'd wheeled in front of you, locking you in his gaze while demonstrating a frenetic series of moves ending with one arm thrust into the air, index finger extended, you'd have fled—and you'd have been right to do so.

"Disco! Disco!" the mangy man would have cackled, hot on your heels. "It is prophesied! The brotherhood of disco will emerge in the Year of the Cat! It is prophesied! *The brotherhood of disco is coming!*"

"Look, punk," you might have called, unintentionally stumbling onto the name of disco's future opposition, "where will this 'brotherhood' come from?"

"From Down Under," he'd have said, staring ominously at the sidewalk. "Where it is hot."

"You mean hell?"

"I can say no more."

"Wait, don't go!"

But even if, before being swallowed by the crowd, the shaman had offered up one more clue, would you have understood?

"The answer is in my Gibb-erish."

"In your . . . ?"

In reality, no one could have predicted it. During a two-year period beginning in July 1977, Barry, Robin and Maurice Gibb, three brothers from Manchester, England, by way of Brisbane, Australia, scared the Bee-Gees-us out of us. In a Beatles-like, Elv-ish chart takeover unparalleled during the seventies, songs written by the Bee Gees held the number one spot in *Billboard* for an incredible thirty-six weeks—a little over a third of the time.

The Gibbs' winning streak was not quite a record—Elvis Presley had hip-thrusted his way to a staggering sixty-seven weeks at number one during the two years beginning in March 1956—but it was nonetheless astonishing. After all, this was the Bee Gees, a band with nothing in their long career that would have pegged them as future kings of the dance floor. Prior to 1975's *Main Course,* the group had been best known for Robin Gibb's melancholy vibrato (which seemed to expand and contract in rhythm) and finger-in-the-ear delivery (which suggested he was perpetually saddled with the toughest harmonies), and for well-crafted if depressing singles like "How Can You Mend a Broken Heart," "I Started a Joke," "Lonely Days," and their first hit (whose subtitle might have worked just as well on one of their later disco anthems), the laugh-a-minute "New York Mining Disaster 1941 (Have You Seen My Wife, Mr. Jones)."

Sometime after Al Green's transcendent 1972 cover of "How Can You Mend a Broken Heart," Robert "RSO" Stigwood, the Bee Gees' manager, began thinking about mixing a little soul into the brothers' mopery. By the time he moved on that strategy, it was 1974, and the band's most recent hit, "Run To Me" (a kind of gloomy "You've Got a Friend"), had peaked almost two years earlier. The last straw appears to have been *A Kick in the Pants Is Worth Eight in the Head,* the inexplicably titled Bee Gees album you never heard. Stigwood felt strongly enough about the nonviability of, uh, let's call it *Pants,* that he was willing to risk postponing the release of a new Gibb disc by well over a year, a lifetime in those days. He hired a new producer—legendary Atlantic Records staffer Arif Mardin—and the refreshing result was *Main Course.* J-j-j-jump-started by the breathy blueblood soul of "Jive Talkin'," the album hinted at a strange future in which the Bee Gees would get down with their formerly not-very-bad selves. Mardin, who would later resuscitate Chaka Khan's career, would never again helm a Bee Gees record, but he had eased the Brothers Gibb on down the road to disco fame (and record-shattering infamy).

In 1976, after *Main Course* had run its course, and before Stigwood accepted the assignment of finding soundtrack fodder for a certain upcoming disco movie, the Bee Gees unwittingly prepped themselves for Travolta-mania with a single-only release called "You Should Be Dancing." With its air-sucking hi hat, invocations to dance, and deep thoughts ("she's juicy"), the orphan single was unapologetically disco, and eventually found a home on the *Saturday Night Fever* soundtrack. (The fact that the chorus opened with an indecipherable line that sounded like, "Whatcha doin' when you're in a cup," proved immaterial.) The next Bee Gees album, *Children of the World* (1976) produced three hits: "Boogie Child," "Edge of the Universe," and "Love So Right."

Cut to 1977. It's hard to say how *Saturday Night Fever* would have fared without the Bee Gees' music, just as it's pure speculation to guess how the music would have fared without the film; the two are ultimately inseparable. *Fever*'s opening image—of former Sweathog John Travolta as a sidewalk-strutting Brooklyn hardware-store employee—is inseparable from the infectious groove of "Stayin' Alive": its thumping bass drum, its burbling guitar, its faux Philly strings. In any case, it was the gorgeous "How Deep Is Your Love" that actually launched the *Fever* soundtrack, knocking "You Light Up My Life" off the top of the charts after an agonizing ten-week crisis in national taste. That was only the beginning. During the week of March 18, 1978, "Stayin' Alive" and the infectious "Night Fever" were numbers one and two, respectively, with Samantha Sang's Gibb-penned "Emotion" in the third spot. ("Emotion" prompted debate as to whether Sang was actually a slowed-down recording of the Bee Gees, but conspiracy theorists were silenced when it was revealed the artist was actually an old Australian friend of the brothers. She was given the song as a gift [a free-gee?] at a time when the Gibb formula couldn't miss. Cannibalized by "Night Fever," "Emotion" stalled at number 3. It would be the last Top 40 hit Samantha sang.)

Hawaiian chanteuse Yvonne Elliman also enjoyed some low-grade *Fever,* scoring her own number one with "If I Can't Have You," written by the Bee Gees. Tavares went Top 40 with yet another *Fever* Gibb-let, "More Than a Woman," although the Bee Gees' own lighter-than-air recording of the song (misheard by our friend D.T. as "Banana Woman") was superior. And in July 1978, even as Stigwood's most recent brainchild, the heretical *Sgt. Pepper* movie, was tanking, Frankie Valli's Barry Gibb–penned title song for the film version of *Grease* was on its way to number one. Carol Douglas covered "Night Fever." Candi Staton covered "Nights on Broadway." Rare Earth covered "Warm Ride." Fellow Aussie Olivia Newton-John recorded Barry and Robin's "Come On Over." Even the Boston Pops' Arthur Fiedler got into the act with 1979's *Saturday Night Fiedler.*

The Bee Gees' franchising efforts were thriving on another front—the home front—in the form of a kid brother. Andy Gibb was a mere boy, a wee Gee, at the time of his siblings' first success (he was nine in 1967, the year of "New York Mining Disaster"), too young in those pre-Hanson days to be a pop star. But ten years later, with the help of his brothers, Andy defined the mainstream summer of '77 with "I Just Want to Be Your Everything," and, at the height of *Saturday Night Fever* fever, landed a seven-week number-one hit with "Shadow Dancing," a Bee Gees discard. A victim of his overnight success, the youngest Gibb died at age thirty in 1988.

After exhausting the *Fever* soundtrack, temporarily the best-selling album of all time, the Gibb brothers released *Spirits Having Flown* (1979). The album shot to number one and added "Too Much Heaven" (a worthy sequel to "How Deep") and "Tragedy" to the Bee Gees canon. A double greatest-hits package capped the winning streak, selling into the millions despite the fact that almost everyone on the planet already owned *Saturday Night Fever.*

They were called Bee Gees because of the confluence of *B*'s and *G*'s in their early career: they had been the Brothers Gibb; they had been the Brisbane Gibbs; and, when they were still known as the Rattlesnakes, they had gotten help from both benefactor Bill Good and deejay Bill Gates. In 1979, when the disco backlash began in earnest, other combinations were suggested: "bubble-gum"; "boogie geeks"; in Maurice's case, "balding guy." (Pop fans save their nastiest vitrol for their guiltiest pleasures.)

In 1980, Barbra Streisand recruited Barry Gibb as a writer-producer, and *Guilty,* essentially a Bee Gees album with Babs's vocals, proved to be the last Gibb-family smash of the era. After that, pop-cultural amnesia set in and the world forgot about the Brothers Gibb, now the blacklisted guys, who couldn't escape their disco legacy until 1989 ("One"). Even then, the public was reluctant to forgive (themselves?), and the group wouldn't score again for nine years. (Note: John Travolta fared no better against the anti-disco forces, languishing in near-oblivion after 1983's *Stayin' Alive*—the *Fever* sequel—until Quentin Tarantino came a-pulpin'.)

None of this was particularly fair. From the beginning, the Bee Gees had been good pop writers, with a better-than-good vocal blend and a remarkable bead on America's tastes. If disco, on the whole, sucked, the Bee Gees proved the genre could support invention, even sweetness. They had hands in producing several of the best nonrock records of their time, and they stayed the (main) course, surviving ups and downs that would have ruined lesser trios. All of which casts doubt on our mangy street prophet's anti-Gibb disco prophecies; if we're going to blame anyone for the "brotherhood of disco," let's blame K.C., whose stinky "Boogie Shoes" also appeared on the *Fever* soundtrack. (Why stigmatize the Sunshine Band leader any further? You have to ask?)

The Linen

SOFT ROCK

"I'd Really Love to See You Tonight" • England Dan & John Ford Coley
(Big Tree, 1976)
"Shannon" • Henry Gross (Lifelong, 1976)
"You Are the Woman" • Firefall (Atlantic, 1976)
"Sometimes When We Touch" • Dan Hill (Thea Century, 1977)
"When I Need You" • Leo Sayer (Warner Bros., 1977)
"I Just Want to Be Your Everything" • Andy Gibb (RHO, 1977)
"I Go Crazy" • Paul Davis (Bang, 1977)
"Can't Smile Without You" • Barry Manilow (Arrest, 1978)
"Just When I Needed You Most" • Randy Van Warmer (Bearsville, 1979)
"Sad Eyes" • Robert John (EMI America, 1979)

In June 1976, a group of recording artists including "England Dan" Seals, John Ford Coley, Eric Carmen, Leo Sayer, and Dan Hill (dubbed "the Maudlin Squad") gathered in Bleeding Heart, California, to celebrate their shared musical vision. "Alda-mont," as the event became known, was presided over by then president Jimmy Carter, who presented the inaugural Gloomy Gus award to Barry Manilow, the artist whose work "best exemplifie[d] extraordinary vulnerability and neediness." Accepting for the absent maestro of melancholy was Henry Gross, still in mourning over the loss of his dog. Choking back tears, he read a telegram from Manilow: "To my dear colleagues . . . Can't smile without you."

Okay, none of the above is true, but there *was* a loose affiliation of sulky songsmiths that thrived in the late 1970s.

Mindful of gas shortages and the need for energy conservation, pop radio gave unprecedented leeway to adrenaline-free popsters like Paul Davis ("I Go Crazy"), Kenny Nolan ("I Like Dreamin'"), and America ("Today's the Day"). The artists' sound was an even lighter take on the "baby I'm-a want you" MOR of the early seventies—leavened Bread, if you will—and their songs can still be heard today, as originally recorded, in dental offices and grocery stores: they have become Muzak versions of themselves.

Firefall, a soft-rock supergroup with a lineup that included once-and-future members of Spirit, Jo Jo Gunne, the Byrds, Heart, and the Flying Burrito Brothers, were the genre's nature boys. Hailing from Colorado, they were kings of the mellow frontier, with albums featuring proto–New Age artwork—a comet falling across a night sky, a full moon reflected off the ocean—and sickly-sweet ditties like "You Are the Woman" and "Just Remember I Love You." But the boys from Boulder were not the only ones simulating sincerity in the studio: Paul Davis (no relation to Mac) out-Manilowed Manilow on "I Go Crazy," and was rewarded with an unprecedented forty weeks on *Billboard;* Randy Van Warmer (née Van Wormer) struck gold with "Just When I Needed You Most"; Andy Gibb went to number one with brother Barry's "I Just Want to Be Your Everything"; and David Gates unbroke Bread for the lightly milquetoasted "Lost Without Your Love." (Like most of their Maudlin Squad brethren, Firefall would go into free fall in the eighties, stymied by a tougher, meaner America that showed less patience for "wimp rock.")

Few realized that behind their sensitive facades, these melancholy babies were as frisky as the next pop star: some of soft rock's soapiest ballads were in fact underhanded come-ons. (Is that your heart on your sleeve, or are you just happy to see me?) Hot on the heels of Sammy John's "Chevy Van,"

England Dan and John Ford Coley released their passive-aggressive anthem of unrequited lust, "I'd Really Love to See You Tonight." Part of the ever-popular phone-call genre (encompassing everything from Chuck Berry's "Memphis" to Todd Rundgren"s "Hello It's Me"), the song conjured a picture of a hapless dude sitting at home thumbing through his frayed black book of ex-girlfriends, looking for a night's diversion. . . . The call is placed. Leaving no time for even an imaginary response, our Romeo begins, "Hello, yeah, it's been awhile, not much, how 'bout you?" —following with low-cost date ideas, like watching television and walking around. Finally, he delivers one of pop's greatest Mondegreens (misheard lyrics), the first line of the chorus: "I'm not talking 'bout the linen . . ."

What "linen"? The question echoes down through the ages.

Actually, our hero wasn't talking about linen, or bedclothes, or anything of the sort. The lyric actually reads, "not talking 'bout movin' in" (emphasis on the second syllable of "movin'"). It's a "no commitment, no common-law" pitch, and what's wrong with that? The guy's just being honest. He's laying his cards on the table. He's *not* talking 'bout the linen. Aren't Maudlin Squad members allowed to get horny like everyone else?

Actually, no—it's in the bylaws.

But they did. It may have been vulnerable and sincere, but Dan Hill's "Sometimes When We Touch" was still about weeping during intimacy (raise your hand if the honesty was too much for you). Dr. Hook, into their post–Medicine Show, post–Shel Silverstein period, propositioned the world with the tepid "Sharing the Night Together." Leo Sayer, who had sported a clown costume on his 1973 album *Silverbird*, laid it on thick on 1977's "When I Need You": drifting amiably through the country-tinged lullaby, his circus togs a distant memory, Sayer mollycoddled us into thinking he had gone wan, when he was actually Don Juan. When he needs her, he reaches out his hand . . . and . . . ? When he wants love, he just closes his eyes . . . and . . . ?

In the end, it was plain old self-pity that best defined the soft-rock experience. Barry Manilow couldn't "smile without you," Robert John stared into "sad eyes," Peter Cetera worried about what would happen "if you leave [him] now," and Henry Gross mourned his dog, Shannon, who was drifting out to sea. They were rewarded with fame, riches, and a couple of Alda-mont reunions, but these *Love Boat* stowaways seemed to spend much of the late seventies sulking. It wasn't hard to picture each of them home alone, languishing on tear-stained sheets, TV test patterns illuminating the gloom, dishes in the sink, unopened mail in the hall. It was only a matter of time before they would fall out of Top 40 favor, before they would have to get on with their lives—pay those bills, scrub those dishes, and, yes, launder that linen.

Dazed and Confused

ROCK

"Shout It Out Loud" • KISS (Casablanca, 1976)
"The Boys Are Back in Town" • Thin Lizzy (Mercury, 1976)
"Walk This Way" • Aerosmith (Columbia, 1976)
"(Don't Fear) The Reaper" • Blue Öyster Cult (Columbia, 1976)
"Night Moves" • Bob Seger (Capitol, 1977)
"Who Are You" • The Who (MCA, 1978)
"Lay Down Sally" • Eric Clapton (RSO, 1978)
"You Really Got Me" • Van Halen (Warner Bros., 1978)
"Don't Do Me Like That" • Tom Petty & the Heartbreakers (Backstreet, 1979)
"Fool in the Rain" • Led Zeppelin (Swan Song, 1979)

When Pope John Paul II played Yankee Stadium in 1979, he joined a growing list of big stars who were packing sports facilities in North America. Sure, the pontiff's backstage refreshments were different from Aerosmith's, and his entourage was dressed more conservatively (almost no halter tops), but rock concerts and religious road shows shared a propensity for grand gestures, ritual, and above all, spectacle.

By 1976, rock was all about spectacle. That year, The Who became the first band to use lasers in concert. Kiss's Gene Simmons breathed fire and spit blood. Pink Floyd launched a giant inflatable pig. Elton John dressed like an interplanetary Liberace. Ted Nugent's show incorporated trapeze stunts; ELP's, an enormous hydraulic drum riser. Earnest, sixties-style rock was all but extinct—"Everybody was a little tired of peace and love," says Alice Cooper—and the era of the stadium megashow had arrived.

, Enter KISS, a New York City quartet whose painted faces, pyrotechnics, and cartoonish personae made a non-issue of an uninspired catalog consisting of workmanlike anthems ("Shout It Out Loud") and calculated crossover ballads ("Beth"). Touring and recording relentlessly during the late seventies (1978 saw all four members release platinum solo albums), Kiss spawned spin-offs such as a made-for-TV movie called *KISS Meets the Phantom of the Park,* and two best-selling Marvel comic books. Meanwhile, the KISS Army, a fan club with many thousands of male members (pun intended), found a seemingly limitless supply of new recruits in thrill-starved Middle America. This was more than style over substance; this was suburb over style.

Aerosmith had more in common with blues-based groups like Led Zeppelin and the Rolling Stones than with KISS, but their audience was similar. Shooting to fame in 1976 with the twin Top Ten attack of "Dream On" and "Walk This Way" (again, the ballad/anthem combination), Aerosmith was a fixture on the arena circuit until its original lineup began to splinter in 1979. Simultaneously, Zep and the Stones continued to attract capacity crowds, touring on midcareer milestones like *Presence* and *Some Girls.* Other rock stalwarts crowding the concert scene included Eric Clapton, returning to form with *Slowhand;* the Who, on the tail end of what Pete Townshend calls "the equipment-smashing period"; and shock-rock pioneer Alice Cooper, still icky after all those years.

The Astrodome-ification of rock was not without its detractors. Pink Floyd's Roger Waters declined to play stadiums after 1977. Frank Zappa questioned the viability of playing music in halls "designed for basketball." And certainly the trampling deaths of eleven general-admission ticketholders at a Who show at Cincinnati's River Front Coliseum in 1979 didn't reflect well on the concert business.

Then there was the blockbuster syndrome, a bigger is better mentality that had infected all of entertainment. "Event" tours, then as now, tended to crowd out small-scale expeditions by lesser-known or first-time acts—how could an intriguing Be-Bop Deluxe–City Boy double bill, for example, compete with a Supertramp or Genesis show its intended audience would sooner die than miss?

But the marginalization of a Be-Bop Deluxe—or, for that matter, a Little Feat or a Tom Waits—did not trouble the moguls Pink Floyd's David Gilmour liked to call "dickheads." There was big money, *unprecedented* money, at stake. By 1975, rock records accounted for 80 percent of the music market, a staggering statistic to those who remembered the soundtrack- and standards-driven pre-rock period. Labels, driven to arrogant extremes by surging profits, glided remorselessly forward, sharklike, enjoying one of the most avaricious periods in the history of the music business. (As the joke goes, that's why they don't call it the "music music.")

Which is not to suggest the late seventies lacked for truly classic rock—great work is possible, even when commercial stakes are high. "Night Moves," Bob Seger's inspired expedition into memory, teenage lust, and the heart of Saturday night, was by turns poignant and propulsive, and turned out to be the jewel in the blue-collar rocker's crown. Led Zeppelin's "Fool in the Rain" —from the plain-brown-wrapped, final Zep LP, *In Through the Out Door*—was a revelation; all thundering shuffle and sinewy, octave-deep guitar. Thin Lizzy's "The Boys Are Back in Town," a back-slappin', street-fightin', summer-reunion anthem, was Springsteen via Dublin, and frontman Phil Lynott's finest hour. The title track from

1978's *Who Are You* showcased the fifth-gear glory of the original Who roster for what would prove to be the last time: drummer Keith Moon died of a drug overdose shortly after the album's release. Also notching evergreen guitar hits were the Stones ("Beast of Burden"), the Eagles ("Life in the Fast Lane"), Queen ("We Will Rock You"), and Blue Öyster Cult ("[Don't Fear] The Reaper").

Among the new voices of the period, Tom Petty and the Heartbreakers stood out. "Don't Do Me Like That" (1979), a punkishly intense meat-and-potatoes rock song, was the band's first big hit. Ten years later, Petty had achieved alternative-Dylan status.

Heavy metal, thought by many to be a dead issue, began to reemerge as a commercial force in 1978 and 1979, when AC/DC's quadruple-platinum *Highway to Hell* was released, and Van Halen, Judas Priest, and the Scorpions hit the U.S. charts for the first time. Women, too, became part of the picture; not just traditional rock sirens like Grace Slick or Heart's Wilson sisters (Ann and Nancy), but so-called "jailbait acts" like Suzi Quatro and the Runaways (featuring Joan Jett). Successful rock films of the day included the Ramones' *Rock 'n' Roll High School,* Led Zepplin's *The Song Remains the Same,* and The Who's *Quadrophenia* and *The Kids Are Alright.* Southern rock endured, with Molly Hatchet, ZZ Top, the Charlie Daniels Band, the Marshall Tucker Band, and the ill-fated Lynyrd Skynyrd going platinum or better. Northern (read: Canadian) rock increased its commercial presence with new albums by BTO, Loverboy, Triumph, April Wine, Rush, and Mahogany Rush (no relation).

The strands were everywhere; late-seventies rock was pluralistic almost to the point of disintegration. Nonetheless, rockers of all stripes were galvanized by clear opposition: the evil empire called Disco. "Our goal . . . was to destroy disco," says Petty. The disco boom would go bust soon enough, but in May 1979, even as the cream of rock's old guard (Paul McCartney, George Harrison, Mick Jagger) was jamming at Eric Clapton's wedding, the *Billboard* Hot 100 remained crowded with dance-floor doodads by the likes of Donna Summer, Chic, and the Village People. It was lasers and flashpots versus mirror balls and strobe lights, *Cat Scratch Fever* versus *Saturday Night Fever,* and clearly the battle wasn't over yet. Disco's uptown attitude, three-piece polyester suits and gay supporters constituted a major affront to the rock ideal, and Gene Simmons's growing army of fans was in no mood to kiss and make up.

No Static At All

STEELY DAN

"Kid Charlemagne" • Steely Dan (ABC, 1976)
"The Fez" • Steely Dan (ABC, 1976)
"Haitian Divorce" • Steely Dan (ABC, 1976)
"Green Earrings" • Steely Dan (ABC, 1976)
"Peg" • Steely Dan (ABC, 1977)
"Home at Last" • Steely Dan (ABC, 1977)
"Deacon Blues" • Steely Dan (ABC, 1978)
"FM (No Static At All)" • Steely Dan (MCA, 1978)
"Josie" • Steely Dan (ABC, 1978)
"Here at the Western World" • Steely Dan (ABC, 1978)

"The great roe," writes Woody Allen, "is a mythological beast with the head of a lion and the body of a lion, though *not the same lion.*"

Is there, in all the world, a better description of Steely Dan, the 1970s' notoriously reclusive studio duo? Probably, but let's try to make this work anyway. The roe is a physically unremarkable creature whose contradictions are invisible to the naked eye; likewise, Walter Becker and Donald Fagen's non-image image gave no indication of their startling, duplicitous songwriting. The roe is mythical (i.e., its very existence is questionable); the press-shy Becker and Fagen, who stopped touring for two decades starting in 1974, cultivated J. D. Salinger–style invisibility. For the roe, duality (head/body) is fundamental; ditto the Dan (rock/jazz). Both creatures spring from familiar traditions—the roe is a relative of the faun (goat/human), and the Dan started out as a Top 40 band—but ultimately defy our expectations. Finally, there's the thread of ironic humor that defines both: Allen's roe is a seemingly academic tidbit that turns out to be a joke, and Steely Dan was a serious rock-and-roll outfit named after a milk-squirting dildo (from the, er, seminal novel *Naked Lunch*).

To this day, people often miss the humor in Steely Dan. But the now-regrouped duo's work was funny, funnier by far than the best Ray Stevens or the worst William Shatner. From bawdy lyrical barbs like "I may never walk again" to musical gene-splices like the jazzed-up reggae of "Haitian Divorce," they delighted in foisting their darkly comic vision on an unsuspecting public, though never to the point of craving belly laughs; as Becker points out, "There's a fine line as to how funny a song can be before it goes over the line into the Spike Jones/Dr. Demento kind of area." A song about wearing a condom ("The Fez"), then, written at the height of the seventies swinging-singles era, is funny only if no one's sure exactly what it means. A song about a bordello ("Here at the Western World") works best if it's made up of discrete, pinpoint details. "FM (No Static At All)" bites the hand that feeds it, but ever so gently.

Steely Dan was not always a studio-only songwriting partnership; until the mid-seventies, it was a performing band, with a roster, gigs, and bearded roadies. In those days, the Dan would appear on television (*American Bandstand, The Midnight Special*), play opening slots for the likes of Bread and the Guess Who, and even occasionally respond to record-company pressure for a new LP, but as Becker and Fagen tired of the road and embraced the full possibilities of the recording studio (as the Beatles had done after *Revolver*), the rock model became irrelevant, and band members began to scatter—two to the Doobie Brothers, several to oblivion.

Post-1974, the flow of hit singles temporarily dried up, but Steely Dan's legend continued to grow. Becker and Fagen became pop's Stanley Kubricks—auteurs working in secrecy on meticulously crafted masterworks (like *Katy Lied* [1975] and *The Royal Scam* [1976])—and single-handedly kept the spirit of jazz alive in the mainstream, to the chagrin of orthodox rock fans. Labeled "hippie Muzak" and "cocktail rock," accused of being "too perfect," the duo (with co-conspirators Gary Katz and Roger Nichols) nonetheless forged ahead, putting its supernatural spit-polish on überpop like "Kid Charlemagne" and "Green Earrings."

By mid-1976, *Newsweek* was touting Steely Dan as "the best American rock group of the seventies," and sessions for another album were under way in Los Angeles. *Aja,* finally released in October 1977, substantially expanded Becker and Fagen's sonic palette and harmonic vocabulary, not to mention their fan base, and bore three American hits: "Peg," a galloping, plagal blues of intoxicating freshness; "Josie," a plea for the return of the Motorcycle Girl (like *Rumblefish* if Mickey Rourke's character were female); and "Deacon Blues," maybe the Dan's lushest, most emotional song ever.

The album's seven longish tracks buried disturbing ideas in gorgeous melodic settings, à la Randy Newman. The doomed jazzman of "Deacon Blues," the drug-ravaged lover of "Black Cow," and the exotic locales of "Aja" all had antecedents on previous Steely Dan albums, but this time around, the overall level of the songwriting, production, and arrangements had gone a notch higher—from A to A-plus—making *Aja* pretty much the best record in the solar system.

Sales cleared the one million mark. Grammy nominations

rolled in. A 1978 tour was planned, though the cost of bring-
ing what Becker called "the enlarged band" on the road ultimately proved prohibitive. Warner Brothers wooed the duo
away from ABC, even as power broker Irving Azoff was signing on as manager.

With *Aja*'s singles still on the charts, the Becker-Fagen
theme song to the proto-*WKRP* movie *FM* climbed to number
22. Big-band legend Woody Herman recorded five Dan tunes
on *Chick, Donald, Walter and Woodrow*. Becker and Fagen
became producers, helming an album for jazz saxophonists
Warne Marsh and Pete Christlieb (Christlieb had recently improvised his way through the tags of "Deacon Blues" and
"FM"). A two-record Dan *Greatest Hits* package, released for
the 1978 Christmas rush, went platinum immediately, consol-
idating the gains of the previous twelve months.

The above developments changed Becker and Fagen's pri-
orities not at all. If they were now on equal commercial foot-
ing with Boston, Foreigner, and the Eagles (all co-stars on the
FM soundtrack), they remained at odds with the music industry's capricious star system. At decade's end they were
still at work on *Aja*'s follow-up, and their recording pace since
Gaucho (1980) has been slower than Pete Rose's trip to
Cooperstown. Notorious for their endless overdubbing—
eight guitarists, all giants, tried the solo on "Peg" before Jay
Graydon's was approved—they have gone down in pop history as crazed perfectionists.

But Steely Dan's records were not bereft of spontaneity.
Tracks like "Home at Last" and "The Royal Scam" were simply
collections of the best spontaneous moments from many,
many takes—not a bad definition of a successful recording
session. Becker and Fagen brought an engaging, detached
swagger to rock and roll, injecting the then floundering genre
with fresh harmonic information (including the infamous "μ

major" chord), unprecedented studio smarts, and a precocious, format-straddling bravado. ("A band like Steely Dan couldn't get arrested now," says former Dan guitarist Jeff "Skunk" Baxter. "Are you AC? Are you AOR? Are you CHR?") Their seamy, vaguely apocalyptic lyrical scenarios probed the dustiest corners of the American consciousness, exuding a cynicism appropriate to an era in which a disgraced ex-president could command $600,000 plus 10 percent of the profits for a television special (David Frost's *Interviews with Nixon*).

That Becker and Fagen have not spawned as many imitators as their contemporaries is a testament to the complexity of their pristine bebop-pop; it's music that requires real technical facility to reproduce. But the frequency of Dan samples in contemporary recordings (from De La Soul to Lord Tariq and Peter Gunz) indicates a continued relevance. The "thinking fan's Top 40 band" never aspired to Beatles-like dominance, after all. Steely Dan were happiest locked in their laboratory, removed from the annoying requirements of stardom, synthesizing beat poetry and dance beats, scornful rants and prewar song forms, rock and jazz. They were Boz Scaggs without the ballads, David Bowie without the wardrobe, 10cc without the snickering. Like the great roe, they were comfortable in the realm of the absurd, head and body just slightly out-of-sync. And they are still visible—well, audible, anyway—down the FM dial, under the banyan trees, in the place where black humor meets white radio.

$250/Hour: Steely Dan by Numbers

- Number of studio musicians used on *Aja:* 35.
- Number of books in print on the Beatles: ~200; on Steely Dan: 2.
- Number of takes it took drummer Steve Gadd to "rip through" his legendary solo on "Aja": 1.

- Rank of "Haitian Divorce" among all U.K. Steely Dan singles: First.
- Number of Steely Dan albums per year, 1972–77: 1.
- Number of years between *Gaucho* (1980) and *Two Against Nature* (2000): 20.
- Ratio of *Aja*'s budget to *The Royal Scam*'s: 10:1.

Sax and Violins

CORPORATE JAZZ

"Breezin'" • George Benson (Warner Bros., 1976)
"Come Dancing" • Jeff Beck (Epic, 1976)
"Europa (Earth's Cry Heaven's Smile)" • Gato Barbieri (A&M, 1976)
"Birdland" • Weather Report (Columbia, 1977)
"Gonna Fly Now (Theme from *Rocky*)" • Maynard Ferguson (Columbia, 1977)
"*Roots* Medley" • Quincy Jones (A&M, 1977)
"Feels So Good" • Chuck Mangione (A&M, 1978)
"Street Life" • The Crusaders (MCA, 1979)
"Rise" • Herb Alpert (A&M, 1979)
"Morning Dance" • Spyro Gyra (Infinity, 1979)

Jazz rock's evolution into "contemporary jazz" in the mid-seventies is a study in the way the music business assimilates innovators and replicates their work minus the warts. It's a long way from the brittle electric jams of Miles Davis's *Bitches Brew* (1969) to the smooth instrumental soul of George Benson's *Breezin'* (1976), but there is a discernible thread: both albums feature jazz players tackling mainstream, electric idioms. And while Benson is the first to admit he strayed from the jazz religion and bedded the harlot Pop, *Breezin'* was a triple-platinum, number one album full of lengthy, jazz-tinged, partly improvised tunes, and, unless you're Wynton Marsalis, it's hard to call that heresy. It might even be progress.

Like many of the instrumental artists who hit the jackpot in

the post–*Bitches Brew* period, Benson was an established
jazz star long before contemporary jazz existed (or, at least,
was named). He was an acknowledged heir to the Wes Mont-
gomery/Kenny Burrell school of jazz guitar, and a sideman to
many of the genre's giants, which meant precisely nothing to
the rank-and-file, "I know what I like" pop fans who bought
Breezin' in numbers sufficient for it to outdistance the
Rolling Stones. The point was, Benson had distilled his musical spirit into a marketable package; he was the artist who
achieved the first true jazz-pop fusion. To this day, *Breezin'*
remains the principia of contemporary jazz.

Other instrumental success stories of the period included
flugelhornist Chuck Mangione, whose "Feels So Good" made
the Carpenters sound edgy; Gato Barbieri, the Argentine
tenor saxophonist whose *Caliente!* included, uh, hot remakes
of Santana's "Europa" and Marvin Gaye's "I Want You": Spyro
Gyra, the Buffalo-based combo whose hit "Morning Dance"
sounded like a segue from news into weather; the hard-
funkin' Crusaders, jazz's answer to KISS (each member had a
solo album out in 1978 or 1979); trumpeter Maynard Ferguson, whose lovably excessive screeching made "super-C" the
holy grail of high-school jazz ensemble back rows everywhere;
and Herb Alpert, whose "Rise" was his biggest hit since the Ti-
juana Brass went south.

Weather Report's constantly shifting roster found its most
commercial incarnation on the gold record *Heavy Weather,*
with the much-covered "Birdland" winning new fans for Joe
Zawinul's seven-year-old group. Rock guitar god Jeff Beck got
the fusion bug, turning out *Blow by Blow* and the even better
Wired in quick succession. All around were signs of success:
the Grammy Awards created a "Best Fusion Performance"
category; pop-jazz found its way into TV themes (*Barney
Miller, Starsky and Hutch,* and others); and artists like

Beck, Benson, and Mangione began to show up in year-end sales surveys.

Whether all this was good for jazz was the subject of some debate. Purists claimed the proliferation of light-fusion fare was ruining America's one indigenous art form. While jazz legends lived on in the worlds of dance (Alvin Ailey's *Pas de Duke*) and musical theater (*Ain't Misbehavin'*), they were largely absent from the new cast of corporate radio faves. Charles Mingus, Errol Garner, Stan Kenton, and Paul Desmond had recently died, and the survivors weren't worthy of their legacies, went the argument. In a world obsessed with *Roots,* much of the new jazz felt rootless.

Hyperbole was rampant. Hit records by jazz musicians were considered by jazz fans a conflict of interest on a par with the United States' $10 billion arms deal with Iran. "The two camps [rock and jazz] were so orthodox then," observes Joni Mitchell. For contemporary-jazz proponents like Quincy Jones, the new sound was an outgrowth of a shrinking musical world. "The typical [jazz] musician today . . . has listened to and been a part of many other forms of music," wrote Jones in 1976; jazz musicians were influenced by the Beatles and James Brown, just as rock bands like Steely Dan and Chicago were influenced by Sonny Rollins, Thelonious Monk, and the swing tradition. A typical contemporary-jazz record was steeped not only in traditional jazz, but in rock, soul, Latin, funk, and MOR.

Critic Robert Christgau called the result "background music without the foreground," and, in its uninspired moments, contemporary jazz *was* a kind of musical wallpaper—Muzak with better chords. But the best recordings of the new genre found musicians reaching beyond the traditional borders of jazz—George Benson called it "searching for an audience"— and blazing a lucrative trail up the pop charts. Hardcore jazz-beens still claim it was all a travesty, but Weather Report's

Grammy-winning *8:30,* the Pat Metheny Group's *American Garage,* the Crusaders' *Free as the Wind,* and Michael Franks's *Sleeping Gypsy* argue eloquently that the late seventies' fusional delusions were well worth the controversy.

PASSION PLAYERS: The All-Seventies Contemporary Jazz Team

- **Saxophone:** David Sanborn, Tom Scott, John Klemmer, Gato Barbieri, Wayne Shorter, Grover Washington Jr., Stanley Turrentine, Wilton Felder, Ronnie Laws
- **Guitar:** George Benson, Al DiMeola, Larry Carlton, Jeff Beck, Steve Khan, Lee Ritenour, Earl Klugh, Eric Gale, John McLaughlin
- **Keyboards:** Joe Sample, Herbie Hancock, Chick Corea, Bob James, McCoy Tyner, George Duke, Ramsey Lewis, Keith Jarrett, Joe Zawinul
- **Trumpet/Flugelhorn:** Freddie Hubbard, Chuck Mangione, Herb Alpert, Donald Byrd, Maynard Ferguson, Miles Davis
- **Vocal:** Al Jarreau, Michael Franks, Randy Crawford, Patti Austin, Bobby Caldwell, the Manhattan Transfer, Steely Dan
- **Drums:** Billy Cobham, Harvey Mason, Narada Michael Walden, Lenny White, Stix Hooper, Tony Williams
- **Composer/Arrangers:** Quincy Jones, Deodato, Claus Ogerman, Don Sebesky
- **Bass:** Jaco Pastorius, Stanley Clarke, Ron Carter, Miroslav Vitous
- **Flute:** Hubert Laws, Herbie Mann, Bobbie Humphrey
- **Electric Violin:** Jean-Luc Ponty
- **Groups:** Weather Report, Pat Metheny Group, Return to Forever, Spyro Gyra, the Crusaders, the Brecker Brothers, Dixie Dregs, Stuff, Passport, the Jeff Lorber Fusion

The Clinton Administration

FUNK

"Get Up Offa That Thing" • James Brown (Polydor, 1976)
"Play That Funky Music" • Wild Cherry (Epic, 1976)
"Tear the Roof Off the Sucker (Give Up the Funk)" • Parliament (Casablanca, 1976)
"Get the Funk Out Ma Face" • The Brothers Johnson (A&M, 1976)
"Sweet Thing" • Rufus (ABC, 1976)
"Fopp" • Ohio Players (Mercury, 1976)
"Brick House" • Commodores (Motown, 1977)
"One Nation Under a Groove—Part 1" • Funkadelic (Warner Bros., 1978)
"I Wanna Be Your Lover" • Prince (Warner Bros., 1979)
"Rapper's Delight" • Sugarhill Gang (Sugarhill, 1979)

When NASA's *Voyager* probes indicated in 1979 that the Jovian moon Io was the solar system's most volcanically active body, residents of Ohio must have been skeptical: Some very hot funk had been erupting from Dayton (the Ohio Players, Slave, Zapp, Sun); Cincinnati (the Isley Brothers, Bootsy's Rubber Band); Youngstown (Robert "Kool" Bell); Mansfield (Switch); and Steubenville (Wild Cherry). Surely Io's sputtering mountains had nothing on "Fire," "Fight the Power," and "Play That Funky Music." Surely there was no deep-space equivalent of William "Bootsy" Collins ("Psychoticbumpschool"). Musically, Ohio was as molten as it gets.

Funk was the bass- and drum-driven "hard soul" style that had emerged from James Brown's melodically spare mid-sixties sides, and had started in earnest in 1970 when Larry Graham took his thumb to the bass on Sly and the Family Stone's "Thank You (Falettinme Be Mice Elf Agin)." It was music that used the whole band—vocalists, horn section, everything—as a rhythm instrument. Of course, it wasn't an entirely Ohio-centric phenomenon; the genre's other stars hailed from at least a dozen American cities. But it made perfect sense that the heaviest concentration of major-label funk stars was to be found in the grinding, smoggy atmosphere of the industrial Midwest. Less "singerly" than soul, taken less seriously than rock, funk was nuts-and-bolts music for dancing and sex, worlds away from the pristine, poppy R&B emanating from Philadelphia and Miami at the time. The Philly sound was dance music with a studio orchestra; funk was soul on steroids.

If Earth, Wind and Fire (see next chapter) were funk's biggest commercial force, George Clinton was its spiritual leader. With two full-time bands (Parliament *and* Funkadelic) keeping frenzied recording schedules, and a host of side projects like Zapp and the Brides of Funkenstein filling in the blanks, the funk auteur with the peroxide afro was omnipresent, and singles like "Tear the Roof Off the Sucker (Give Up the Funk)" and "One Nation Under a Groove—Part 1" were among the era's most influential.

Parliament/Funkadelic—the two bands were essentially the same, though there was more of Clinton's sci-fi philosophy ("cosmic slop") on the Funkadelic side—gave over-the-top concerts that featured lavish sets and outrageous wardrobe elements like nine-inch-high metallic platform shoes. Whether Clinton was the extraterrestrial prophet he (jokingly?) claimed to be was debatable; for one thing, he appeared to have been born in the not-particularly-otherworldly environs of North Carolina. But pyramid power, "funkativity," and galactic politics weren't, finally, the point; Clinton and company are legends (not to mention Rock and Roll Hall of Fame inductees) because they made deep, gritty, stinky-ass, Limburger-strength funk for the ages. Less well known than Earth, Wind and Fire, less wealthy than many of the hip-hop acts that have sampled them in recent years, they are nonetheless rich in other ways; as Clinton once proclaimed, "Funk is its own reward."

Meanwhile, James Brown, who had been playing funk in the 1960s before it had a name, kept sharing his "latest outlooks" with an increasingly disinterested public (none of his late-seventies albums cracked the Top 100). His "Get Up Offa That Thing" was nonetheless one of the most intense almost-disco singles of the era. Like Clinton, Brown spawned multiple musical offshoots: the JBs, and Fred Wesley and the Horny Horns, both had albums on the charts in the mid-seventies. Brown's indirect musical descendants included Los Angeles's Brothers Johnson, New York's Cameo, Chicago's Rufus (with the brilliant Chaka Khan), Buffalo's Rick James, Oakland's Tower of Power, and Jersey City's Kool and the Gang, whose "Funky Stuff," "Jungle Boogie," and "Hollywood Swinging" set the standard for mainstream funk.

Also descended from James Brown were the Sugarhill Gang, an Englewood, New Jersey, rap group whose groundbreaking 1979 hit "Rapper's Delight" became the template for eighties hip-hop (rap is often traced back to Brown's 1974 single "The Payback"). When it first reared its swelled head, rap was a lark; "Rapper's Delight" seemed no more important in the pop pantheon than, say, Reunion's equally verbose novelty hit, "Life Is a Rock (But the Radio Rolled Me)." But in the years that followed, rap gave voice to the American inner city, putting the means of production squarely in the hands of its street-level practitioners. Sugarhill Records remained at rap's forefront into the 1980s, releasing influential crossover hits like Grandmaster Flash and the Furious Five's incendiary "The Message."

In the meantime, funk had gathered disciples faster than Reverend Sun-Myung Moon. Its influence was felt in the realms of Motown (Marvin Gaye's "Got to Give It Up [Part 1];" Stevie Wonder's "You Haven't Done Nothin'"), jazz (Herbie Hancock's "Chameleon;" the Crusaders' "Feel It"), old-school R&B (the Bar-Kays' "Shake Your Rump to the Funk;" Johnny "Guitar" Watson's "A Real Mother for Ya"), even comedy (*Bill Cosby Is Not Himself These Days [Rat Own, Rat Own, Rat Own]*).

Seduced by funk's propulsive rhythms (and by the Commodores' uncanny ability to make "house" rhyme with "cows"), white America came along for the ride. Mainstream acts like Chicago and Elton John began cutting funk-by-number tracks—"Boogie Pilgrim," indeed. Though Donny and Marie were still more popular than *Soul Train,* and radio apartheid was alive and well, the walls were starting to crumble. With Prince's career and Michael Jackson's second wind already under way, America would soon find itself in an environment where separating "pop" and "R&B" would come to seem arbitrary and artificial—not to mention *un*funky.

A KOOL MILLION: Top Funk Artists 1976–79

Rank	Artist	Hit 45s	Gold 45s	Hit LPs	Gold LPs	Plat. LPs	Multiplat.	Grammys
1	Earth, Wind and Fire	9	5	4	4	4	4	6
2	Parliament/Funkadelic	3	3	7	8	3	0	0
3	Commodores	10	0	6	1	1	0	0
4	Rufus/Chaka Kahn	7	1	4	4	1	0	0
5	Brothers Johnson	3	2	3	3	3	0	1
6	War	2	1	3	4	1	0	0
7	L.T.D.	2	1	3	3	1	0	0
8	Average White Band	1	0	5	3	1	0	0

Funk the World

EARTH, WIND AND FIRE

"Can't Hide Love" • Earth, Wind and Fire (Columbia, 1976)
"Getaway" • Earth, Wind and Fire (Columbia, 1976)
"Serpentine Fire" • Earth, Wind and Fire (Columbia, 1977)
"Best of My Love" • The Emotions (Columbia, 1977)
"Fantasy" • Earth, Wind and Fire (Columbia, 1978)
"Got to Get You into My Life" • Earth, Wind and Fire (Columbia, 1978)
"September" • Earth, Wind and Fire (ARC, 1978)
"Boogie Wonderland" • Earth, Wind and Fire with the Emotions (ARC, 1979)
"After the Love Has Gone" • Earth, Wind and Fire (ARC, 1979)
"In the Stone" • Earth, Wind and Fire (ARC, 1979)

M iss Walton taught Jeff biology in the tenth grade. She was one of the "cool teachers," and her bionic good looks inspired many a schoolboy crush. The fact that she was unmarried gave her the slightest whiff of attainability (or was that just the Bunsen burners?); on the other hand, she was a teacher. This contradiction was compelling to her male students, who were in the throes of biological changes far more dramatic than any on the syllabus.

On a winter afternoon in early 1979, Jeff heard the music of Earth, Wind and Fire pouring out of Miss Walton's car window as she steered deliberately through the school parking lot and passed him with a wave and a toot. Earth, Wind and Fire! That was them, all right, the seventies' funk-pop gods, "Bah-dee-yah"-ing their way through "September," and Miss Walton, a *teacher,* had the volume cranked. Jeff, who had recently mended his broken heart with extended Earth, Wind and Fire (EWF) listening sessions, was spellbound.

Two years after "the parking-lot incident," as it came to be known, EWF were touring in support of their overlooked double album, *Faces,* and a rare stop in Toronto was announced. Though no longer his teacher, Miss Walton got wind that Jeff and his buddy John were going to the show; she was going, too, and offered to give them a ride. Bliss.

The big night came. After a whispered bargaining session about who would sit where, the two boys got into the car. John took the front, and Jeff, having agreed they would trade in the unlikely event that Miss Walton offered a return trip, took the back. Soon the three sidled up alongside Maple Leaf Gardens, and agreed to meet back at the car after the concert. *She was going to drive them home.*

Inside, the EWF multimedia extravaganza highlighted the band's strongest material, including nearly all of *All 'n All* (1977), *The Best of Earth, Wind and Fire, Volume I* (1978), and *I Am* (1979). In addition to spectacular musicianship, lavish lighting, and a pyramid-power set, the show included large-scale magic tricks designed by bunny-toothed illusionist Doug Henning. The musicians, sporting kaleidoscopic robes, spangled bell-bottoms, and multicolored headbands and sashes, looked like an interplanetary wrestling team.

Back in the sixties, EWF leader Maurice White had been a session drummer at Chess Records. He and brother Verdeen convened the original band lineup in 1970. By the late seventies, EWF had defied the "eight is enough" rule—there were ten full-time members—and White had his own Columbia Records imprint (ARC, featuring Deniece Williams, Weather

Report, and the Emotions) and production clients (Barbra Streisand, Valerie Carter, Ramsey Lewis, Neil Diamond, and the Emotions).

Earth, Wind and Fire, so named because White's astrological chart contained no water signs, had a rhythm section that could make the dead dance, an impossibly tight horn section that could cut glass, and the world-class vocal tandem of White and Philip Bailey (the best falsetto voice this side of Russell Thompkins). It was like a hybrid of Parliament, the Stylistics, and Steely Dan, and despite the oft-repeated knock that White and his cohorts were merely making funk "safe" for Top 40, the results were never less than exhilarating. Take "Serpentine Fire," which snaked its way up the charts in 1978: its churning, one-of-a-kind groove and sidewinding horn line were the year's happiest noise. (Even as EWF laid down the funkiest tracks this side of James Brown, they could also outballad the competition with slower fare like "Can't Hide Love" and "Be Ever Wonderful.")

The glorious surprise of seeing EWF live during their peak years was that, with or without Doug Henning, they could match and even surpass their immaculate recordings. Their lighter-than-air music sounded even better in the lighter-in-the-air atmosphere of Maple Leaf Gardens, and they damn near melted the ice beneath the temporary wood floor that night in Toronto. Burning through "Getaway," "Fantasy," "Saturday Night," and "In the Stone," they were relentless, pausing only for White's obligatory kalimba (African thumb piano) solo.

And somewhere down below, in that sea of dancing bodies, was Miss Walton. John and Jeff were at least fifty rows up, near the second blue line (in Canada, arena seats are always identified in relation to the hockey rink), but *la belle femme biologique* was a mere ten rows from the stage with her date, a mystery man who hadn't picked her up nor, apparently, planned to take her home.

"GUESS THE GUY DOESN'T HAVE A CAR," shouted John over the music. Guess not, thought Jeff. Or—could it be?— maybe there was no date. What if Miss Walton was there alone? What if *they* were her date? The thought hung in the air for a moment before the band launched into "After the Love Is Gone," Larry Dunn's tinkling piano signaling 17,000 people to sit down.

Two hours later, Jeff and John navigated through the post-concert throngs to the car, and found Miss Walton leaning against the driver's-side door with a big old bionic grin on her face. On the way back to the suburbs, she popped in a tape, and the car filled with "bah-dee-yah"s and memories of "the parking-lot incident." Jeff, in the front seat, decided then and there that Miss Walton had attended the concert alone, and that her offer to taxi her two former students into the city had not been entirely unselfish. Sure, she looked like Lindsay Wagner, but that was no guarantee she would always have company.

Jeff was dropped off first. As he thanked Miss Walton and stepped out of the car, he left the door open for his friend. "I'm hoping for a kiss good-night," John whispered as he eased into the front seat. The slamming car door choked off Philip Bailey midway through the gorgeous "Reasons," and Miss Walton—not just one of the cool teachers but quite possibly the coolest teacher ever—pulled out of the driveway with a wave and a toot. John, whose "thumbs-up" emerged from the passenger window as the car drove off into the brisk night, settled into his bucket seat, and, riding high on the boundless optimism only Earth, Wind and Fire can instill, planned his next move.

The Doobie Brother

BOB MARLEY

"Roots, Rock, Reggae" • Bob Marley & the Wailers (Island, 1976)
"Exodus" • Bob Marley & the Wailers (Island, 1977)
"Waiting in Vain" • Bob Marley & the Wailers (Island, 1977)
"Jamming" • Bob Marley & the Wailers (Island, 1977)
"Punky Reggae Party" • Bob Marley & the Wailers (Island, 1977)
"One Love/People Get Ready" • Bob Marley & the Wailers (Island, 1977)
"Three Little Birds" • Bob Marley & the Wailers (Island, 1977)
"Is This Love" • Bob Marley & the Wailers (Island, 1978)
"(You Gotta Walk and) Don't Look Back" • Peter Tosh (Atlantic, 1978)
"Satisfy My Soul" • Bob Marley & the Wailers (Island, 1978)

"There's nobody getting into a Jamaican thing," Paul Simon told *Rolling Stone* in 1972. The New Jersey-born composer of the then recent reggae-tinged hit "Mother and Child Reunion" was bemoaning his countrymen's lack of appreciation for Jamaica's latest indigenous art form, and at the time he was right (righteous, even). But four years later, with rockers from Eric Clapton to Steely Dan tackling reggae, and Bob Marley and the Wailers' *Rastaman Vibration* in the American Top Ten, the situation had changed considerably; reggae was resplendent, the genre of the moment, and the only world music going, so far as the U.S. audience was concerned.

At reggae's center, then as now, was Bob Marley. The thirty-one-year-old was more than just Jamaica's biggest star (in rock terms, he was Bob Dylan, the Beatles, the Rolling Stones, and, yes, Paul Simon all rolled into one)—he was a political lightning rod, a religious icon, and a national hero. A devotee of Rastafarianism, the Afro-Caribbean religion that prophesied the deliverance of the black race by a godlike king—specifically, Ethiopian emperor Ras Tafari Makonnen (Haile Selassie I)—he was scrutinized in his homeland at every step with *Columbo*-like thoroughness; some said his opinions could decide an election. In Kingston, the poverty-ravaged Jamaican capital, he was the voice of youth, the "rude boy' from Trench Town (a vast west-side slum) who had risen to prominence through his joyous, muscular art.

Lost at times in the rapturous devotion to Marley was his prowess as a songwriter. By turns tender ("Waiting in Vain") and angry ("Exodus"), playful ("Punky Reggae Party") and devout ("One Love"), he was successfully able to straddle the line between proselytization and confessional. His political exhortations contained nary a false note, and his one-on-one scenarios never lacked for realism and soul. Pretty good for a man whose music at first sounded so strange to rock-trained Northern ears; in reggae, the drummer emphasizes the off-beats, the guitarist never solos, and the groove is slightly "back," or behind the beat (perhaps evidence of Kingston's killing heat).

Marley eclipsed contemporaries like Black Uhuru, Toots and the Maytals, and former cohort Peter Tosh, but that may have been for the best; no one but a bona fide megastar could have opened so many doors so quickly (reggae-by-committee wasn't going to work for an audience weaned on commercial behemoths like *Frampton Comes Alive!* and *Saturday Night Fever*). Reggae, itself a hybrid of Jamaican folk idioms and American R&B, was compelling only if you set your inter-nal clock well below 120 beats per minute (the standard disco tempo). Even Clapton, who had had a number one with Marley's "I Shot the Sheriff," admitted to an initial difficulty understanding "this real loose thing"; until the mid-seventies, musicians of Clapton's vintage had associated Jamaica mainly with ska, a blisteringly quick, almost polkalike dance style light-years removed from the draggy, deliberate hum of reggae.

Not incidental in reggae's Stateside success were two ingredients key to almost any new rock-related style: drugs and hair. Rastafarians considered smoking marijuana ("ganga") a sacrament, and so did many American teenagers. The current "War on Drugs" was no more than a border skirmish in those days, and the legalization movement had the whiff not of pseudo-radical flakiness, but of historical inevitability. Hairwise, Rastafarianism advocated the never-been-combed style called "dreadlocks," again for religious reasons—a verse in *Leviticus* forbids "making baldness upon [the] head"—and a

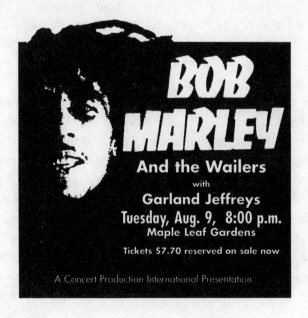

BOB MARLEY
And the Wailers
with
Garland Jeffreys
Tuesday, Aug. 9, 8:00 p.m.
Maple Leaf Gardens
Tickets $7.70 reserved on sale now

A Concert Production International Presentation

quick peek at any seventies high-school yearbook will confirm the appeal of infrequent haircuts.

Still, until 1976, reggae was to music what soccer was to sports: extremely popular in Europe, Africa, and South America, but marginal in the U.S. and Canada. Bob Marley and the Wailers' breakthrough album, *Rastaman Vibration* (1976), contained "Roots, Rock, Reggae," the band's only *Billboard* Hot 100 single, and galvanized their North American following. Melodic, yet unabashedly religious and political, it created reggae awareness in Framptonland overnight.

At home, *Rastaman Vibration* led to "Smile Jamaica," a free concert to be held in Kingston in December 1976. The weeks leading up to the show (and, significantly, a national election) saw an increase in local violence, including an unsuccessful attempt on Marley's life, but the artist nonetheless performed a short set in defiance of his enemies. Soon afterward, Marley and his band went to London to record *Exodus* (number 20, 1977), where exposure to the punk scene yielded the bridge-building single "Punky Reggae Party." "Jamming," *Exodus*'s biggest hit, contained the line, "no bullet can stop us now," a reference to the assassination attempt. *Kaya,* the double live *Babylon by Bus,* and *Survival* (originally titled *Black Survival*) followed, as did international vindication: In 1978 Marley received the United Nations' Medal of Peace. He was lionized by Stevie Wonder on 1980's "Master Blaster (Jammin')," just a year before dying of cancer at age thirty-six in Miami.

Today, Bob Marley's work remains reggae's touchstone. His birthday (February 6) is a national holiday in Jamaica. His music is synonymous with a spiritually centered, relaxed approach to life. His sometimes intimate, sometimes apocalyptic songs attract new listeners daily, in every corner of the world. *Legend,* an Island greatest-hits package, is one of the most popular catalog albums in print, in any genre. Songs like "Waiting in Vain" and "One Love," though not American hits, are among the most-performed in the rock-era canon. But Marley's most lasting legacy may be the still-fresh recognition by First World pop culture that there are other entire musics out there waiting to be discovered—that Youssou N'Dour, for example, deserves as much attention as the English-speaking artists who champion him, that the Western listener is not, as Jamaicaphile Paul Simon might have put it, "an island."

Meltdown

PUNK

"God Save the Queen" • The Sex Pistols (Warner Bros., 1977)
"Rockaway Beach" • The Ramones (Sire, 1977)
"Blank Generation" • Richard Hell and the Voidoids (Sire, 1977)
"Psycho Killer" • Talking Heads (Sire, 1977)
"Lust for Life" • Iggy Pop (RCA, 1977)
"I Fought the Law" • The Clash (Columbia, 1978)
"Because the Night" • Patti Smith (Arista, 1978)
"Love Song" • The Damned (Chiswick, 1979)
"Broken English" • Marianne Faithfull (Island, 1979)
"Town Called Malice" • The Jam (Polydor, 1979)

"Rock & roll is a communicable disease," quoth the *New York Times* in 1956, and Cold War America, spooked by the contagious strain of youthful exuberance carried by Elvis Presley, Little Richard, et al., was inclined to agree. Alarmist rhetoric was everywhere: the new music was variously linked to premarital sex, drug abuse, and juvenile delinquency. Many who liked Ike (Eisenhower) fretted that the day of leather-clad, hip-shaking thugs and cigarette-smoking, knocked-up girlfriends was at hand. Then, abruptly, the Twist, *American Bandstand,* and surf music dispelled such fears. The Heartbreak Hotel went into receivership; the Sugar Shack opened for business. Rock and roll went to $eed, and it would be years before it became truly dangerous again.

By 1976, rock's first bloom was a distant memory—background music for *Happy Days*—and the stars of its second bloom were either dead legends (Hendrix, Joplin) or seasoned celebrities (Jagger, McCartney). A new generation of guitar bands eyed their wealthy, creatively faltering predecessors with deep suspicion. CBGB and Max's Kansas City, two lower-Manhattan rock bars, became the East Coast's nerve center for several of the most important of these artists: Blondie (fronted by ex–Playboy Bunny Deborah Harry), Tom Verlaine's Television (including future Voidoid and punk couture icon Richard Hell), Patti Smith, Talking Heads, and the Ramones.

When the latter two bands toured Britain in 1976, the punk explosion began in earnest. Opinions vary on exactly how much the Ramones/Heads visit influenced the already percolating London scene, but this much is clear: Very soon afterward, English punk became the world's most incendiary music. Rip-'n'-pin fashion, spiky hair, slam-dancing, ritual spitting, BBC bans, and small-scale rioting followed. What else followed? Almost every rock critic on the face of the earth.

The Sex Pistols, a quartet assembled in 1975 by the opportunistic London boutique owner and hypemonger Malcolm McLaren, were punk's most infamous (and critically beloved) band. Exploding in 1976 with a cacophonous single called "Anarchy in the U.K.," and later going to number one on the British charts with a cacophonous album called *Never Mind the Bollocks, Here's the Sex Pistols,* the Pistols left a deliberately ugly smear on popular music that has yet to be cleaned up.

Hailed by Elvis Costello as "the first actual English rock-and-roll singer" and lionized by Neil Young on 1979's "My My, Hey Hey (Out of the Blue)," Sex Pistols frontman Johnny Rotten vilified his queen, his country, his peers—he once called

Sting "evil"—and forever put a face to England's disenfranchised youth. Per the Young song, however, his career was meteoric. After an ill-fated 1978 tour of the U.S., with "bassist" Sid Vicious well into a self-destructive/homicidal downward spiral, the Sex Pistols disbanded, whereupon Rotten [now John Lydon] convened PiL (Public Image Ltd.), his less-than-thrilling new anti-band.

The Pistols, of course, were not lone gunmen. Punk spawned a host of like-minded bands (Dead Boys, Damned, Generation X, The Jam, Buzzcocks, Gang of Four) and related styles (ska, electropop, second-generation rockabilly). Former Mick Jagger attaché Marianne Faithfull returned to the scene with a coarse, hoarse opus called *Broken English*. English superstars David Bowie and Marc Bolan embraced the new music's brash spirit. Punk's impact was considerable. It's worth noting, though, that whereas the British Invasion of the mid-sixties produced at least five truly great rock bands

(Beatles, Stones, Who, Kinks, Yardbirds), British punk produced only two—U2, more or less invisible until 1980; and the
Clash.

Sown from the same seeds as the Sex Pistols (London's
rock scene and Britain's ominous swing to the right), the
Clash made rock anthems for people who hated the idea of
rock anthems. Led by guitarist-composers Joe Strummer and
Mick Jones, the band recorded at least a dozen songs (including "London Calling" [1979] and "Rock the Casbah" [1982])
that still work outside the context of the political/racial/ideo-
logical strife that inspired them. The Clash also eventually
broke big in America—more than you could say for most of
the U.K. snot-and-vitriol quartets—and promptly experienced a backlash from the very fans who had championed
them on the basis that they should bloody well be big in
America. *(Plus ça change . . .)*

Meanwhile, back in the U.S., a phalanx of brainy and/or
goofy punk bands was entrancing critics and savaging rock
convention. David Byrne's Talking Heads were saying what
they meant in such fresh ways that nobody thought they
meant what they were saying; the "brothers" Ramone were
playing fast and dumb; Patti Smith was keeping the genre safe
for urban poets (and being ruthlessly parodied by comedi-
enne Gilda Radner as "Candy Slice" on *Saturday Night
Live*); Black Flag, the Dead Kennedys, and X were energizing
the Left Coast; and Iggy Pop was enjoying newfound patriar-
chal status.

Not that American radio noticed; the closest thing to a *Bill-
board* punk hit during the late seventies was "Because the
Night," Patti Smith's collaboration with Bruce Springsteen, or
Talking Heads' cover of Al Green's "Take Me to the River." The
Ramones' "Rockaway Beach" peaked at number 66. The Po-
lice's "Roxanne" went Top 40, but not by much. And the

British "hard punk" bands were hitless, perhaps by design (the Clash sailed uncharted waters until 1980). The only number one record from the original CBGB scene was Blondie's "Heart of Glass," an ingratiating disco confection that made Donna Summer sound like Mahalia Jackson.

Why all the fuss, then? Was punk merely a scam, fueled by ear-splitting guitars, cut-rate bondage gear, and outrageous stage names like Billy Idol, Jimmy Zero, Poly Styrene, and Rat Scabies? Was it rock's indomitable spirit, tearing out of the seventies' constrictive clothing like a mild-mannered Bruce Banner mutating into the Hulk? Was it, as Paul McCartney suggested, just "another style with good fashion and a good attitude?" Putting aside the question of technical ability—the fact is, many punk bands couldn't (or wouldn't) play very well—punk's agenda seemed to be

- to bring to people's attention the smug, greed-driven state of popular music (not a surprise to anyone who had seen the *Sgt. Pepper's Lonely Hearts Club Band* movie);
- to question the necessity of high-gloss production (the Ramones' debut LP was made for around $7,000, less than one percent of Fleetwood Mac's *Tusk* budget); and
- to expose political corruption and social ills (the Clash) and/or argue the futility of even bothering to fight them (the Sex Pistols).

In the end, Johnny Rotten had about as much effect on the British monarchy as Joan Baez had on Richard Nixon. As Lester Bangs pointed out in *NME* in 1977, music consisting of unmitigated nihilism is "somehow *insufficient*"; pop is supposed to have more charm and humor than an anti-government leaflet. It's true that several voices originally associated with punk (Elvis Costello, Joe Jackson, Sting, David

Byrne, Andy Partridge) became some of the best new song-writers of the eighties, and on that basis alone, maybe the whole mess was worth it. As for where *Never Mind the Bollocks, Here's the Sex Pistols* ranks in the pantheon of classic albums, well, ask anyone. Except a rock critic.

ANTI-MATTERS: Five Unsolved Mysteries of the Punk Era

1) Is the queen, in fact, a "human bein'?"

2) Given the excess of bodily fluids involved in the punk lifestyle, wouldn't "Sid *Viscous*" have been more appropriate?

3) Did American radio stations actually blacklist punk, or did they simply notice that most of it sucked?

4) How many angels can dance on the head of a safety pin?

5) If the Ramones/Talking Heads tour of England in 1976 had been a Styx/Boston tour, would "Anarchy in the U.K." have been a power ballad?

A Flock of Haircuts

NEW WAVE

"Rock Lobster" • B-52's (Warner Bros., 1979)
"Making Plans for Nigel" • XTC (Virgin, 1979)
"Roxanne" • The Police (A&M, 1979)
"Sultans of Swing" • Dire Straits (Warner Bros., 1979)
"Cool for Cats" • Squeeze (A&M, 1979)
"Is She Really Going Out with Him?" • Joe Jackson (A&M, 1979)
"Heart of Glass" • Blondie (Chrysalis, 1979)
"Driver's Seat" • Sniff 'n' the Tears (Atlantic, 1979)
"I Don't Like Mondays" • Boomtown Rats (Mercury, 1979)
"My Sharona" • The Knack (Capitol, 1979)

Many a one-hit wonder surfed in on the so-called "new wave" that crashed on these shores in the late seventies. Though a lucky few rode that initial swell for several hits, the wave attracted more than its share of marginal talents, ill-equipped to "hang five." By the time Gary Numan had abandoned his car and Flash and the Pan had fulfilled their stated destiny, the seas were slick with hair gel, and the beach called pop was littered with the skinny ties and pointy-toe shoes of an army of (mostly English) wipeouts.

And overhead, A Flock of Seagulls hovered.

The best surfers did eventually make it to shore, and thereafter, new wave became a brilliant disguise for some of the era's most important new songwriters.

But "new wave" was as much about fashion as music. The

Knack, a pop band by any other standard, was touted by Columbia, one of thirteen labels that had bid on them, as a "new wave" signing. Why? Because they wore skinny ties and cigarette-legged pants. "My Sharona," The Knack's (and 1979's) biggest hit, was tied to the venerable rock tradition of playing guitar to "get chicks"; there was nothing new about it. (The *Meet the Beatles* configuration on the album cover further emphasized the band's ties to the old wave.)

Sometimes an artist's barber seemed to set the agenda: many bands used hair as a source of identity, almost as a logo. Blondie was named after Debbie Harry's platinum lid. The B-52's were named after the nuclear-warhead hairstyles worn by band members Cindy Wilson and Kate Pierson. Sting, Andy Summers, and Stewart Copeland—collectively the best rock band of the late seventies—dyed their hair blond for a 1978 Wrigley's Gum ad and decided to maintain the dye job as part of their Police "uniform."

The B-52's mix of fifties camp and sixties psychedelia—"Rock Lobster" still sounds like something from *The Jetsons*—made their eponymous 1979 LP an entertaining anachronism. Fred Schneider, part carnival barker and part Bob Barker, was the flamboyant, Frankenfurter-like host of the party, and his songs were perfect for the "pogo," perhaps the least-complex dance step in history (you jump up and down).

The Police, essentially an outlet for Sting's songwriting talents, merged rock and reggae on *Outlandos d'Amour* (1978) and *Reggatta de Blanc* (1979). *Outlandos'* "Roxanne" was a U.S. hit, its off-kilter drum pattern and dry-as-bones guitar hinting at grooves to come, but *Reggatta's* even better "Message in a Bottle" stalled at number 74 despite going to number one in the more Brit-aware environs of Canada. Sting would eventually guide the Police to post–new wave superstardom.

Joe Jackson, a former music-composition major troubled by

a world in which "pretty women" cavorted with "gorillas," wrote prickly, ironic songs that reminded some critics of Elvis Costello. To be sure, there were similarities: a waiflike, non–pop star presence; an angry vocal edge; a supremely poppy yet punkish sensibility; and an eclectic spirit camouflaged by some very direct, guitar-driven pop. That spirit would eventually lead Jackson into multiple styles—jump-swing on 1981's *Jumpin' Jive;* Latin pop on 1982's *Night and Day;* chamber music on 1999's *Symphony No. 1*—and make him impatient with the superficial, extramusical demands of the video age. Luckily, that was only after he had committed to vinyl gems like "Sunday Papers," "It's Different for Girls," and "Breaking Us in Two."

Like Jackson, the English artpop outfit XTC quickly outgrew the increasingly nonspecific "new wave" label. Their "Making Plans for Nigel" (1979), a middle-finger salute to the English class system and an American FM favorite, hinted that they were smarter than your average rock quartet. (No one knew how much smarter, though: XTC albums like *Oranges and Lemons* [1989] and *Apple Venus, Volume One* [1999] have since redefined post-Beatles pop.) Squeeze, too, earned Lennon-McCartney comparisons early on (it's entirely possible the Beatles themselves would have been called new-wavers if "I Saw Her Standing There" had come out in 1979), with U.K. hits "Up the Junction" and "Cool for Cats." Stymied

by American tastes, though, Squeeze would, in the eighties, find themselves fighting an impossible-to-explain losing battle for Stateside recognition.

Such was not the case with Dire Straits, guitarist Mark Knopfler's London-based, soon-to-be-platinum blues-rock group. Because of the spare production on *Dire Straits* (1979), the band was considered new wave, though no one could find any similarity between the lead guitar–spattered "Sultans of Swing" and Devo's "Mongoloid." Other notable nearly new-wave singles included Cheap Trick's "Surrender"; Sniff 'n' the Tears' "Driver's Seat"; Japan's "Quiet Life"; the Monks' "Drugs in My Pocket"; the Cars' "Just What I Needed" (a rare example of New England wave); and the Boomtown Rats' "I Don't Like Mondays." ("Mondays," future Band Aid organizer Bob Geldof's epitaph for the victims of a 1979 school shooting in San Diego, immortalized the killer's disturbing answer to the question of why she'd shot eleven people. The girl's parents attempted to have the song banned in the U.S., which may explain why it stalled at number 73 in *Billboard,* but went to number one in England.)

When the dust settled, new wave's early proponents had either distanced themselves from the style, or disappeared altogether. The less-is-more production style of The Police and Company endured, though, influencing eighties releases as different as Prince's "When Doves Cry" and Steve Miller's "Abracadabra." Minimalism was the rage. Even the mighty Cadillac was getting smaller. The music industry's plan to declaw punk had worked like a charm; an all-out British invasion had been averted. Those who had abhorred new wave from the start could take comfort: former hairdressers A Flock of Seagulls were on their way back to Liverpool; Blondie had become a generic, full-service pop group; and soon enough, the Stray Cats would strut no more.

Revenge of the Nerd

ELVIS COSTELLO

"Less Than Zero" • Elvis Costello (Columbia, 1977)
"Watching the Detectives" • Elvis Costello (Columbia, 1977)
"Mystery Dance" • Elvis Costello (Columbia, 1977)
"(I Don't Want to Go to) Chelsea" • Elvis Costello (Columbia, 1978)
"Pump It Up" • Elvis Costello (Columbia, 1978)
"Radio, Radio" • Elvis Costello (Columbia, 1978)
"Oliver's Army" • Elvis Costello (Columbia, 1979)
"Accidents Will Happen" • Elvis Costello (Columbia, 1979)
"Cruel to Be Kind" • Nick Lowe (Columbia, 1979)
"A Message to You Rudy" • The Specials (Chrysalis, 1979)

If it's true that punk was nothing more than "young boys dropping their trousers" (and Sir George Martin says it was), Elvis Costello was the exception that proved the rule. With his pigeon-toed, defiant stance, and vitriolic vocal delivery, Costello at first seemed a true punker, the English equivalent of *Network*'s irate newscaster: he was mad as hell, and he wasn't going to take it anymore. But his punk persona turned out to be a brilliant disguise; lurking just behind the bluster was an old-school pop craftsman with a traditional streak a mile wide.

Costello (né Patrick Declan MacManus) fashioned an early career that seemed to exist simply to piss America off. Let us count the ways:

1) He ransacked rock 'n' roll's past, taking Mr. Holly's image and Mr. Presley's name.

2) In an infamous "silly argument" (his description) with Bonnie Bramlett and Stephen Stills, he used the words "blind," "ignorant," and "nigger" in the same sentence to describe Ray Charles.

3) On a *Saturday Night Live* appearance, he stopped partway into "Less Than Zero," saying there was "no reason to do this song," then launched into "Radio, Radio"—a song he had been told not to play.

4) He became notorious for doing short shows and for being rudely dismissive of his audiences (this in the era of the four-hour Springsteen love fest).

As unpleasant as the above sounds, however, punk was peaking—the Sex Pistols had only recently begun wiping their metaphorical—and, for all we know, actual—bums on the Union Jack—and people were getting used to angry posturing. In the end, Costello's most provoking career move was probably his first, the copping of the King's name, a brazen and brilliant attention-getter from the mind of manager Jake Riviera.

After his explosive debut at London's Nashville club in May 1977 (just months before Elvis the First died), Costello turned his attention to *My Aim Is True,* surely among the best two or three debuts in rock's now substantial history. The album opened with the line, "Now that your picture's in the paper being rhythmically admired"—a brilliant pre-*Seinfeld* masturbation euphemism—and escalated from there. A treasure trove of melodic hookery and wry lyrical gems worthy of Ira Gershwin (Gershwin is said to have been baffled by comparisons to Costello following the release of 1982's *Imperial Bedroom*), *Aim* had balladry ("Alison"), reggae ("Watching the Detectives"), pop ("[The Angels Want to Wear My] Red Shoes"), shuffling blues ("Blame It On Cain"), Stones-style rock ("Miracle Man"), and explosive rockabilly ("Mystery Dance"). Beyond Costello's unflinching vocals, the unifying element in this wild eclecticism was the country-tinged playing of Clover, an American combo masquerading as "the Shamrocks" for the twenty-four-hour marathon session.

Nick Lowe, who scored a Stateside hit a couple of years later with his own "Cruel to Be Kind," produced *Aim* and every subsequent Costello album through 1981's underrated *Trust*. It was Lowe, while playing in the "hippie" band Brinsley Schwartz, who had brought Costello to the attention of Stiff Records in the mid-seventies. Apart from these immortal contributions, Lowe eventually bestowed upon Elvis one of his own compositions, the Brinsley Schwartz–era "(What's So Funny 'Bout) Peace, Love and Understanding," which became one of Costello's rare recorded covers and—not incidentally—one of the most guileless rave-ups in pop history.

Readying himself for his sophomore release, Costello formed the Attractions, the angry young rhythm section that would back him for more than a decade. *This Year's Model*, released less than a year after *Aim*, was harder-edged, and delivered on the promise of the first album with E.C. classics like "Radio, Radio," "This Year's Girl," and the spitfire-lyriced "Pump It Up." To this day, *Model* consistently shows up as a favorite in critics' polls, fan forums, and other rock think-tanks.

By 1979, like many of his contemporaries, Costello had been saddled with the "new wave" label. It seemed ridiculously inadequate, much like the "alternative" label he would acquire in the nineties; this was transcendent pop, not alt-rock, and, as if to prove it, the artist released his self-proclaimed "pop-star record," *Armed Forces*, that year. For those who have heard its hookery and semantic intrigue in the intervening years, *Armed Forces* (originally entitled *Emotional Fascism)* has become a standard-bearer for ambitious, lasting popular music. It was on *Armed Forces* that Costello perfected his fusion of darkly comic lyrics and cheerful melodies, a trick that gave his songs a combustible inner tension. Nowhere was this more evident than on the album's anthemic centerpiece, "Oliver's Army," a story of mercenary soldiers, Cold War paranoia, and existential dread, borne on the most triumphant melody since Paul McCartney's "Maybe I'm Amazed" (Costello and McCartney would collaborate a decade later). *Forces'* other catchy downers included "Senior Service," "Green Shirt," and the irresistible "Moods for Moderns."

As Costello began branching out into production (he helmed the Specials' hilarious 1979 debut), the kudos continued. Though he was passed over for a Best New Artist Grammy in favor of the long-forgotten disco duo A Taste of Honey, Costello was beloved by rock critics, who dubbed him "the new Dylan." (If Costello shared anything with Dylan, it was his penchant for lyrically dense, "Positively Fourth Street"–like diatribes.) Thereafter, the albums poured out in quick succession as Costello plumbed his seemingly inexhaustible muse; the tally as of 2000 is twenty albums in twenty-three years.

In a verbal swipe worthy of the artist himself, David Lee Roth accused critics of supporting Elvis Costello "because they all look like him" (i.e., bookwormish, slight, ill-equipped to rock). Even Costello has referred to the "myth of the wimp" when attempting to account for his appeal, and, certainly, an easy-to-decode public persona can get you a couple of years into a music career. But the nerd has more than outlived his image (anyone who could have predicted in 1977 the late-nineties Costello–Burt Bacharach team-up needs to set up a psychic hotline). If he has largely avoided the upper reaches of the *Billboard* charts—*Armed Forces* got to number 10, but none of his seventies singles charted in North America—it does not seem to have dimmed his creative spirit; he has worked in a variety of styles (Memphis soul on 1980's *Get Happy,* country on 1981's *Almost Blue)* and with a variety of stylists (the classical Brodsky Quartet on 1992's *The Juliet Letters,* Bacharach on 1998's *Painted from Memory),* always with exceptional results.

Costello has said of his early songwriting that he was trying "to take some ready-made clichés and come up with . . . photo-negative versions of them." So perhaps the "pretty fingers lying in the wedding cake" in "Alison" are somehow connected to the happy couple in the Dixie Cups' "Going to the Chapel." Perhaps the clumsy, lustful virgins in "Mystery Dance" are rock-and-roll cousins of the sleepy innocents in the Everly Brothers' "Wake Up Little Susie." And perhaps "(Angels Wanna Wear My) Red Shoes" wouldn't have been possible without Carl Perkins's "Blue Suede Shoes." No matter—Costello's "photo-negatives" paradoxically linked him to the very pop tradition he was attempting to turn on its head. Because deep at the core of his worldview was another well-worn cliché that needed no inversion: he knew that only "fools fall in love," and he's spent almost a quarter century trying to explain just why that is.

Conclusion

The final Village People hit of the seventies was "Ready for the 80's." But were we? Record companies were axing insolvent disco acts by the dozen, and KISS had mercifully reached its commercial peak, but those same record companies would soon be bankrolling poseurs like Culture Club, and, as we now know, KISS was far from dead.

The eighties would see the formerly fertile field of pop overgrown with hair metal and Madonna wannabes. Video would kill the radio star. A-ha would be discovered. Tiffany would come to a mall near you. Jefferson Starship would shed the first half of its name and the last shred of its credibility. In 1981, REO Speedwagon would have the number one album in America *for an entire season.* The future, to put it mildly, was not bright.

Of course, the lousy eighties doesn't necessarily mean good seventies; we could be looking backward through "Rose Garden"–colored glasses. As Iggy Pop has observed, people tend to "enshrine whatever it was that was great when [they] were youngest and happiest."

Q. Have your fearless authors reached the age of moribund nostalgia?

A. Undoubtedly.

But the fact that we're fond enough of "the Me Decade" to wax nostalgic about the theme from *Welcome Back, Kotter* doesn't mean we've completely lost touch with reality. Song for song, the seventies are just plain better than their overpaid younger sibling (the eighties). Despite a penchant for secondhand culture like *The Blues Brothers, Beatlemania,* and *Grease,* the decade that taste forgot fostered great originality. Everywhere, there were fresh voices and emerging styles: funk and reggae were born; the Philadelphia and Los Angeles scenes erupted; rock embraced jazz and classical music; Bruce Springsteen, Randy Newman, Joni Mitchell, and dozens of other pop auteurs advanced the art of songwriting—all, miraculously, without the aid of video clips.

In *Precious and Few: Pop Music in the Early '70s,* we argued that the post-Beatles, pre-disco period (1971–75) was an underappreciated, discrete era, devoid of central characters but rich in ensemble-cast variety. In this book we have tried to establish that the late seventies (1976–79) also spawned its share of classics, despite a "bigger is better" mentality (the blockbuster virus) that would eventually destroy the uninhibited mosaic of AM radio. (The blockbuster virus started in the film industry, where mid-seventies crowd-pleasers like *Jaws* and *Star Wars* raised the financial stakes by a factor of ten almost overnight. Spielberg's shark and Lucas's Wookies not only caused an incurable case of opening-weekend fever, but led to the long-term marginalization of the medium-budget, character-driven movies that used to be Hollywood's bread and butter. "In the early seventies," wrote Richard Corliss, "there were more *kinds* of films. In the late seventies . . . there's one majority, melting-pot cinema.")

Music's *Jaws* was *Frampton Comes Alive!*—a multiplatinum juggernaut by a journeyman rocker that, commercially speaking, set the stage for *Rumours, Saturday Night Fever,* and *Grease.* Loosed on a booming economy, *Alive!* touched off a wave of bullish overconfidence in the record business, the likes of which have not been seen since. Corporate mergers, movie spinoffs, vanity labels, and long-term megadeals (a faltering McCartney got $20 million from Columbia) became almost as common on the American landscape as nuclear grain silos. Rock, the music of the counterculture, was packaged as ruthlessly as dish soap. Rock stars, increasingly insulated from their fans, were treated like high-ranking executives. It was what *Rolling Stone* publisher Jann Wenner would call a "period of concession" between music and the music industry.

It was also, not incidentally, the golden age of the double-album cash grab. Formerly a perk reserved for A-list artists at the peak of their powers—the Beatles' White Album, the Rolling Stones' *Exile on Main Street,* and Elton John's *Goodbye Yellow Brick Road* are good examples—twofers were now viewed by labels simply as a way to collect ten bucks instead of five from flush consumers. There were double original soundtracks *(Saturday Night Fever, Grease, FM),* double career retrospectives (from the Beatles, Hendrix, Creedence Clearwater Revival, Steely Dan), even double disco compilations *(Disco Party, Disco Boogie, A Night at Studio 54).* Double live albums proliferated, too, with everyone from Aerosmith to Zappa getting their long-winded ya-ya's out (see Appendix, The Show That Never Ends). Records that actually warranted the extra creative space—records like *Songs in the Key of Life, The Wall,* and *Blue Moves*—were as rare as Satanists at a Debby Boone concert; Donna Summer's streak of four consecutive needlessly double LPs from 1977 to 1979 was far truer to the spirit of the age.

What record companies didn't take into account during their new-artist feeding frenzy was that Frampton, Fleetwood Mac, and the Bee Gees had started in the 1960's British rock scene; by 1976 they were all crafty veterans. No amount of short-term A&R hustle was going to guarantee another *Rumours, Saturday Night Fever,* or *Frampton Comes Alive!* The difference between an artist that naturally produces a smash (say, the Bee Gees) and an artist groomed by a record label to produce a smash (say, Andy Gibb) is considerable, something like the difference between a photogenic child and one who just mugs for the camera. It's why America wasn't CSNY, why the Monkees weren't the Beatles.

And speaking of the Beatles, it was the ill-fated 1978 Beatles "tribute" movie *Sgt. Pepper's Lonely Hearts Club Band,* featuring Frampton and the Bee Gees, that sounded the death knell for the era of unfettered record-industry greed. Despite a couple of worthy covers—Aerosmith's "Come Together" and Earth, Wind and Fire's "Got to Get You Into My Life" still sound good today—the *Pepper* movie and soundtrack (a double LP, natch) crashed faster than the blimp at the Super Bowl in *Black Sunday.* Amid outraged reviews and peals of laughter, the limits of the blockbuster approach were laid bare: the music-business trinity of hubris, cynicism, and titanic greed had, for once, proved fruitless. (The real damage was yet to come, in the remorselessly bottom-line eighties.)

Were the late seventies, then, some kind of golden age? Let's ask the experts. Donald Fagen was "waiting for better

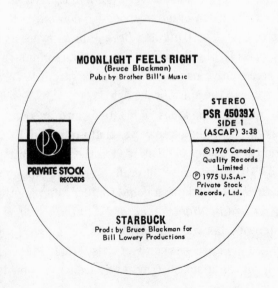

times." Lester Bangs complained of "retreads" and "solipsism." Elvis Costello found himself listening to "monotonous, rootless music." Tom Petty wondered what young musicians would "learn from . . . all that disco."

The late seventies were the beginning of the downslope, a time when rank-and-file pop fans began to understand that the era of progress (for lack of a better word) in popular music was over. Rock and soul had never been unfettered by commerce—Dick Clark's *American Bandstand* was hardly the stuff of revolution—but after 1976, the tail began to wag the dog, the record sellers began dictating policy to the record makers, and the last traces of Beatles-era idealism went up in smoke (from a distant fire). In one stunt that typified the era, Casablanca Records boss Neil Bogart had a life-size cake of Donna Summer flown to New York for a promotional tour in two first-class seats. That's the kind of money-to-burn abandon that lent credence to Pete Townshend's "decline of the Roman empire" remark.

Are you, on the other hand, not charmed by "Afternoon Delight"? Or cheered by "Moonlight Feels Right," a werewolf-friendly party anthem for the ages? Would you not allow that "Stayin' Alive" was brilliant, despite its spoofability? What about "Love Hangover," which is only now getting its due as disco's "Stairway to Heaven"? And fresh hybrids like "Message in a Bottle" (pop/ska), "Birdland" (pop/jazz), and "Bohemian Rhapsody" (rock/operetta)? And *Aja,* and *Silk Degrees,* and *I Am?* Elvis C.? Warren Z.? Chuck E.?

Okay, so maybe "Love Rollercoaster" did little to illuminate what George McGovern called "the poignant condition of our lives in the seventies," and maybe "Boogie Nights" didn't put "beauty and truth and meaning into popular song" (as Ralph J. Gleason had written of Paul Simon in 1966), but the pop scene was still relatively, *residually* healthy until around 1980. For every "Love and Happiness," the brilliant Al Green single that was shut out of the Hot 100 in 1977, there was a "Serpentine Fire" or a "Walk This Way" that *did* succeed. For every country crossover smash (say, "The Gambler") evincing the death of liberalism, there was a "Running On Empty" or a "Prove It All Night." The days of the pan-categorical, kitchen-sink Top 40 were over, but, damn it, about two dozen of the best songwriters in the history of rock were still in the game.

The title of this book comes from "Night Moves," a magical 1976 single by Bob Seger. Reputedly inspired by the film *American Graffiti* (George Lucas's masterpiece about a 1962 long night's journey into day), "Night Moves" was Seger's ode to teen angst, summertime, and making out, sung from the point of view of a white male in his thirties. It rocked, its lyrics rang Springsteen-true (the near-whispered middle section recalled "Jungleland"), and it was all about looking back, which, you'll notice, is also what our books are about. The grown man who starts "humming a song from 1962" in the dead of night as he casts his memory back to the sights and sounds of a rock-and-roll adolescence, is us—just add ten years.

Rock has a long tradition of turning its gaze backward. It's the thread that connects disparate classics like "Penny Lane," "Crocodile Rock," "I Wish," "Late in the Evening," "American Pie," "Hey Nineteen," "Old Days," "Glory Days," and "Keeping the Faith." It's also the foundation of all but the most clinical rock criticism. And (we're pretty sure) it's the reason Springsteen broke into Graceland in 1976, hoping for an audience with the King.

Does true pop nirvana exist only in a remote golden age, five presidents away, current only when it shows up as a sample on some contemporary dance record? Well, okay, maybe not. As much as rock and roll's best days are behind it, and true pop songcraft is an endangered species ("Foolish Games" is a far cry from "What a Fool Believes"), somewhere out there in radioland, right now, an impressionable kid is experiencing the visceral thrill of popular music as a slight but strangely powerful song vibrates through thin air and sinks, whole, into his or her skin, never to be removed. (Perhaps he or she will someday write a tender reminiscence called *Livin' La Vida Loca: Pop Music in the Late '90s.*)

We are the "barely boomers," the children of the Brady years. We saw, as P.J. O'Rourke puts it, hipness collapse into disco. We learned about integrity from Richard Nixon, intimacy from Donna Summer. We bought *Frampton Comes Alive!* in droves, for no reason other than that there were droves of us buying it. We forgot about Stax and embraced Styx. Like the conformist hordes in *Monty Python's Life of Brian,* we screamed, "We're all individuals!" in perfect unison. We were scorched by the disco inferno. We spent the night at the Hotel California. We are family. We are the champions. We write the songs. We just want to be your everything. We love the nightlife, we got ta boogie.

American Graffiti's hot-rodder John Milner is still out there, takin' 'em all on, cruising the warm Southern California night to the strains of Buddy Holly and Fats Domino. Bob Seger's adolescent alter ego is still stealing away "to the backroom, the alley, the trusty woods" with his dark-eyed teenage princess. And we're out there, finding humor and madness and love and the good song on the right station as we roll through the suburbs, Milnerlike, in a gargantuan yellow 1973 Ford station wagon with fake wood paneling on the side. And you? Well, if you followed us this far, you're probably still out there, too. And hey, bub, the light's green.

Appendixes

The Show That Never Ends:

Double Live Albums 1976–79

Aerosmith • *Live! Bootleg*

The Allman Brothers Band • *Wipe the Windows—Check the Oil—Dollar Gas*

Atlanta Rhythm Section • *Are You Ready!*

Average White Band • *Person to Person*

Joan Baez • *From Every Stage*

The Band • *The Last Waltz*

Bee Gees • *Here at Last . . . Bee Gees . . . Live*

George Benson • *Weekend in L.A.*

David Bowie • *Stage*

Jimmy Buffett • *You Had to Be There*

Glen Campbell • *Live at the Royal Festival Hall*

Harry Chapin • *Greatest Stories—Live*

Natalie Cole • *Natalie . . . Live!*

Commodores • *Commodores Live!*

Neil Diamond • *Love at the Greek*

Bob Dylan • *Bob Dylan at Budokan*

Peter Frampton • *Frampton Comes Alive!*

Marvin Gaye • *Marvin Gaye Live at the London Palladium*

J. Geils Band • *Live—Blow Your Face Out*

Genesis • *Seconds Out*

The Grateful Dead • *Steal Your Face*

Al Jarreau • *Look to the Rainbow—Live in Europe*

Jethro Tull • *Jethro Tull Live—Bursting Out*

Kiss • *Kiss Alive*

Little Feat • *Waiting for Columbus*

Lynyrd Skynyrd • *One More from the Road*

Chuck Mangione • *An Evening of Magic—Chuck Magione Live at the Hollywood Bowl*

Barry Manilow • *Barry Manilow—Live*

Bob Marley and the Wailers • *Babylon by Bus*

Dave Mason • *Certified Live*

Bette Midler • *Live at Last*

The Moody Blues • *Caught Live + 5*

Willie Nelson • *Willie and Family Live*

Ted Nugent • *Double Live Gonzo!*

Outlaws • *Bring It Back Alive*

Graham Parker and the Rumour • *The Parkerilla*

Parliament • *Parliament Live/P. Funk Earth Tour*

Teddy Pendergrass • *Teddy Live! Coast to Coast*

Elvis Presley • *Elvis in Concert*

Pure Prairie League • *Live!! Takin' the Stage*

Queen • *Live Killers*

Rainbow • *On Stage*

Lou Rawls • *Lou Rawls Live*

Smokey Robinson • *Smokin'*

Diana Ross • *An Evening with Diana Ross*

Todd Rundgren • *Back to the Bars*

Rush • *All the World's a Stage*

Santana • *Moonflower*

Bob Seger and the Silver Bullet Band • *'Live' Bullet*

Donna Summer • *Live and More*

The Tubes • *What Do You Want from Live*

UFO • *Strangers in the Night*

Village People • *Live and Sleazy*

Wings • *Wings Over America* [triple album]

Neil Young • *Live Rust*

Frank Zappa • *Zappa in New York*

Various Artists • *California Jam 2*

Various Artists • *No Nukes—The MUSE Concerts for a Non-Nuclear Future* [triple album]

The Last Hustle:

Billboard's Last Singles Chart of the Seventies (12/22/79)

The final Hot 100 of the decade contained flotsam and jetsam from the disco era—five Casablanca entries—and many hints of things to come. That Rupert Holmes's "Escape (The Piña Colada Song)" was number one, was only the most obvious indignity.

DISCO

No. 2 "Please Don't Go"/K.C. and the Sunshine Band *[On second thought, do.]*

No. 9 "Ladies Night"/Kool and the Gang *[sic.]*

No. 36 "Yes, I'm Ready"/Teri DeSario with K.C. *[One can never have enough K.C.]*

No. 61 "Move Your Boogie Body"/The Bar-Kays *[Post-Stax hot wax.]*

No. 83 "Second Time Around"/Shalamar

CLASSIC ROCK

No. 10 "Take the Long Way Home"/Supertramp *[Exploding commercially, imploding creatively.]*

No. 14 "Head Games"/Foreigner *[Get it?]*

No. 27 "Damned If I Do"/The Alan Parsons Project

No. 30 "Third Time Lucky"/Foghat

No. 57 "Since You've Been Gone"/Rainbow

No. 64 "Fool in the Rain"/Led Zeppelin *[proto-New jack meets metal.]*

No. 76 "Heartbreaker"/Pat Benatar
No. "99"/Toto

ADULT CONTEMPORARY

No. 6 "Do That to Me One More Time"/The Captain and Tennille *[G-rated lust.]*
No. 7 "You're Only Lonely"/J.D. Souther
No. 15 "Cruisin'"/Smokey Robinson
No. 34 "Déjà Vu"/Dionne Warwick *[A "seen it all before" ballad produced by Barry "Heard It All Before" Manilow.]*
No. 44 "I'd Rather Leave While I'm in Love"/Rita Coolidge
No. 66 "September Morning"/Neil Diamond
No. 77 "Longer"/Dan Fogelberg
No. 92 "With You I'm Born Again"/Billy Preston and Syreeta *[See also Charles Colson.]*

OUT WITH THE OLD

No. 16 "Better Love Next Time"/Dr. Hook *[Love pun #1.]*
No. 28 "Don't Let Go"/Isaac Hayes
No. 31 "Chiquita"/ABBA
No. 42 "Forever Mine"/The O'Jays *[Philly farewell #1.]*
No. 53 "You Know That I Love You"/Santana
No. 63 "Last Train to London"/Electric Light Orchestra *[Wilbury-in-waiting.]*
No. 72 "Working My Way Back to You"/Spinners *[Philly farewell #2.]*
No. 93 "Holdin' On for Dear Love"/Lobo *[Love pun #2.]*
No. 98 "Ready for the Eighties"/The Village People *[That's what you think. . . .]*

IN WITH THE NEW

No. 23 "I Wanna Be Your Lover"/Prince *[Purple reign, year one.]*

No. 25 "Don't Do Me Like That"/Tom Petty and the Heart-breakers *[Roots, rock, year one.]*

No. 33 "I Need a Lover"/John Cougar *[But not as badly as Prince does!]*

No. 43 "Rapper's Delight"/Sugarhill Gang *[Hip-hop, year one.]*

No. 56 "Voices"/Cheap Trick

No. 74 "Message in a Bottle"/The Police

No. 97 "Dreaming"/Blondie

BIRTH OF IRONY

No. 32 "Pop Musik"/M

No. 46 "Video Killed the Radio Star"/The Buggles *[The first video played on MTV.]*

No. 58 "Crazy Little Thing Called Love"/Queen *[Postmodern rockabilly.]*

No. 60 "Money"/The Flying Lizards

GOOD POP MUSIC THAT SUCCEEDED

No. 4 "Send One Your Love"/Stevie Wonder

No. 11 "Rock with You"/Michael Jackson

No. 21 "This Is It"/Kenny Loggins *[L.A. gothic.]*

No. 26 "Wait for Me"/Daryl Hall and John Oates

GOOD POP MUSIC THAT PROVED COMMERCIALLY MARGINAL

No. 75 "You're Gonna Get What's Coming"/Bonnie Raitt

No. 81 "Star"/Earth, Wind and Fire *[In what nightmarishly unjust universe could this song* not *be a smash?]*

No. 82 "Can We Still Be Friends?"/Robert Palmer

DOUBLE DUTY

• Herb Alpert: No. 40, "Rotation"; No. 96, "Rise."

• Commodores: No. 5, "Still"; No. 68, "Wonderland."

- Eagles: No. 17, "The Long Run"; No. 20, "Heartache Tonight."
- Fleetwood Mac: No. 35, "Sara"; No. 52, "Tusk."
- Barry Manilow: No. 29, "Ships"; No. 78, "When I Wanted You."
- Anne Murray: No. 37, "Broken Hearted Me"; No. 67, "Daydream Believer."
- Kenny Rogers: No. 22, "Coward of the County"; No. 94, "You Decorated My Life."
- Styx: No. 3, "Babe"; No. 65, "Why Me." *[Why us?]*
- Donna Summer: No. 8, "No More Tears"; No. 50, "Dim All the Lights."

MISCELLANEOUS

No. 47 "Rainbow Connection"/Kermit the Frog *[Muppet.]*
No. 80 "Memorize Your Number"/Leif Garrett *[Garrett.]*
No. 89 "Volcano"/Jimmy Buffett *[Parrot.]*

Saturday Night Live musical guests, 1976–79

1976: James Taylor, Boz Scaggs, Joe Cocker, John Prine, Kinky Friedman, The Band, Ry Cooder, Paul Simon, George Harrison, Brian Wilson, Frank Zappa, George Benson, Chuck Berry, Leo Sayer, Donny Harper Singers, the Kinks, Richard Buskin, Levon Helm, Dr. John, the Meters, Santana, Tom Waits and Susan Nickerson, Brick, Roslyn Kind, Kate and Anna McGarrigle, Alan Price, Neil Innes, Joan Armatrading, Jennifer Warnes, Kenny Vance.

1977: Jackson Browne, Taj Mahal, Libby Titus, Paul Simon, Ray Charles, Leon Redbone, Willie Nelson, Elvis Costello, Randy Newman, Dirt Band, Bonnie Raitt, Billy Joel, Ashford and Simpson, Art Garfunkel, Stephen Bishop, Eddie Money, Meat Loaf, Eugene Record, Keith Jarrett, Gravity, the Blues Brothers, Jimmy Buffett, Gary Tigerman, Sun Ra.

1978: The Rolling Stones, Devo, Frank Zappa, Van Morrison, The Grateful Dead, the Blues Brothers, Kate Bush, Peter Tosh and Mick Jagger, the Doobie Brothers, Talking Heads, Judy Collins, Delbert McClinton, Eubie Blake and Gregory Hines, the Chieftains, Rickie Lee Jones, Ornette Coleman, James Taylor, Linda Ronstadt and Phoebe Snow, Bette Midler.

1979: Blondie, Bob Dylan, Chicago, Tom Petty, the Roches, Randy Newman, David Bowie, Desmond Child and Rouge, the B-52's, Marianne Faithfull, Gary Numan, Sam and Dave, the

J. Geils Band, James Taylor and Paul Simon, David Sanborn, The Grateful Dead, Anne Murray, the Specials, Amazing Rhythm Aces, Bruce Cockburn, 3-D, Andrew Gold, Andre Crouch and Voices of Unity.

Foreground Music:

Hit Movie and TV Themes, 1976–79

"How Deep Is Your Love" • Bee Gees [number 1; *Saturday Night Fever*]

"Stayin' Alive" • Bee Gees [number 1; *Saturday Night Fever*]

"Night Fever" • Bee Gees [number 1; *Saturday Night Fever*]

"You Light Up My Life" • Debby Boone [number 1; *You Light Up My Life*]

"Welcome Back" • John Sebastian [number 1; *Welcome Back, Kotter*]

"Gonna Fly Now" • Bill Conti [number 1; *Rocky*]

"Grease" • Frankie Valli [number 1; *Grease*]

"Evergreen" • Barbra Streisand [number 1; *A Star Is Born*]

"Car Wash" • Rose Royce [number 1; *Car Wash*]

"Do You Know Where You're Going To" • Diana Ross [number 1; *Mahogany*]

"Theme from *S.W.A.T.*" • Rhythm Heritage [number 1; *S.W.A.T.*]

"*Star Wars* Theme/Cantina Band" • Meco [number 1; *Star Wars*]

"You're the One That I Want" • John Travolta and Olivia Newton-John [number 1; *Grease*]

"Nobody Does It Better" • Carly Simon [number 2; *The Spy Who Loved Me*]

"Last Dance" • Donna Summer [number 3; *Thank God It's Friday*]

"Hopelessly Devoted to You" • Olivia Newton-John [number 3; *Grease*]

"The Main Event/Fight" • Barbra Streisand [number 3; *The Main Event*]

"Summer Nights" • John Travolta, Olivia Newton-John and Cast [number 5; *Grease*]

"Happy Days" • Pratt and McClain [number 5; *Happy Days*]

"Makin' It" • David Naughton [number 5; *Meatballs*]

"Nadia's Theme" • Barry DeVorzon and Perry Botkin Jr. [number 8; *The Young and the Restless,* TV show]

"Copacabana (At the Copa)" • Barry Manilow [number 8; *Foul Play*]

"Got to Get You Into My Life" • Earth, Wind and Fire [number 9; *Sgt. Pepper's Lonely Hearts Club Band,* movie]

"Star Wars (Main Title)" • John Williams [number 10; *Star Wars*]

"Ready to Take a Chance Again" • Barry Manilow [number 11; *Foul Play*]

"Theme from *Close Encounters*" • John Williams [number 13; *Close Encounters of the Third Kind*]

"Goodbye Girl" • David Gates [number 15; *The Goodbye Girl*]

"Oh! Darling" • Robin Gibb [number 15; *Sgt. Pepper's Lonely Hearts Club Band,* movie]

"I'm Easy" • Keith Carradine [number 17; *Nashville*]

"Gimme Some Lovin'" • Blues Brothers [number 18; *The Blues Brothers,* movie]

"Different Worlds" • Maureen McGovern [number 18; *Angie*]

"Baretta's Theme (Keep Your Eye on the Sparrow)" • Rhythm Heritage [number 20; *Baretta,* TV show]

"Prisoner" • Barbra Streisand [number 21; *The Eyes of Laura Mars*]

"FM (No Static At All)" • Steely Dan [number 22; *FM*]

"Thank God It's Friday" • Love and Kisses [number 22; *Thank God It's Friday*]

"Come Together" • Aerosmith [number 23; *Sgt. Pepper's Lonely Hearts Club Band,* movie]

"Greatest Love of All" • George Benson [number 24; *The Greatest*]

"Rainbow Connection" • Kermit [number 25; *The Muppet Movie*]

"Making Our Dreams Come True" • Cyndi Grecco [number 25; *Laverne and Shirley,* TV show]

"Theme from *Close Encounters*" • Meco [number 25; *Close Encounters of the Third Kind*]

"My Fair Share" • Seals and Crofts [number 28; *One on One*]

"Almost Summer" • Celebration, featuring Mike Love [number 28; *Almost Summer*]

"Every Which Way But Loose" • Eddie Rabbitt [number 30; *Every Which Way But Loose*]

"Chase" • Giorgio Moroder [number 33; *Midnight Express*]

"Magical Mystery Tour" • Ambrosia [number 39; *All This and World War II*]

"Good Friend" • Mary MacGregor [number 39; *Meatballs*]

"Ease On Down the Road" • Diana Ross and Michael Jackson [number 41; *The Wiz*]

"Theme from *Charlie's Angels*" • Henry Mancini [number 45; *Charlie's Angels,* TV show]

"Greased Lightnin'" • John Travolta [number 47; *Grease*]

"So Sad the Song" • Gladys Knight and the Pips [number 47; *Pipe Dreams*]

"Can You Read My Mind" • Maureen McGovern [number 52; *Superman*]

"Long Live Rock" • The Who [number 54; *The Kids Are Alright*]

"Easy to Be Hard" • Cheryl Barnes [number 64; *Hair*]

"Theme from *King Kong*" • Love Unlimited Orchestra [number 68; *King Kong*]

"Animal House" • Stephen Bishop [number 73; *Animal House*]

"Through the Eyes of Love" • Melissa Manchester [number 76; *Ice Castles*]

"Mary Hartman, Mary Hartman (Theme)" • Deadly Nightshade [number 79; *Mary Hartman, Mary Hartman,* TV show]

"Theme from *Superman* (Main Title)" • London Symphony Orchestra [number 81; *Superman*]

"You Can't Win (Part 1)" • Michael Jackson [number 81; *The Wiz*]

"Get Back" • Billy Preston [number 86; *Sgt. Pepper's Lonely Hearts Club Band,* movie]

"Gonna Fly Now" • Rhythm Heritage [number 94; *Rocky*]

The Platinum Screen:

Top 40 Movie Soundtracks, 1976–79

1. *Saturday Night Fever*
2. *Grease*
3. *A Star Is Born*
4. *Star Wars* (music)
5. *The Song Remains the Same*
6. *Rocky*
7. *Sgt. Pepper's Lonely Hearts Club Band*
8. *FM*
9. *The Kids Are Alright*
10. *Children of Sanchez*
11. *Thank God It's Friday*
12. *Close Encounters of the Third Kind*
13. *You Light Up My Life*
14. *The Main Event*
15. *American Hot Wax*
16. *The Muppet Movie*
17. *Star Wars* (story)
18. *The Lord of the Rings*
19. *The Wiz*
20. *The Spy Who Loved Me*
21. *Superman*
22. *Quadrophenia*
23. *All This and World War II*
24. *The Rocky Horror Picture Show*
25. *New York, New York*
26. *Hair*
27. *Midnight Express*

28. *Youngblood*
29. *The Deep*
30. *Animal House*
31. *Every Which Way But Loose*
32. *More American Grafitti*
33. *The Buddy Holly Story*
34. *Manhattan*
35. *Pipe Dreams*
36. *Foul Play*
37. *Alien*
38. *One on One*
39. *Rock 'n' Roll High School*
40. *King Kong*

Grammy Nominees and Winners, 1976–1979

List excludes awards outside the scope of this book. "Song of the Year" and "Best Rhythm & Blues Song" awards go to songwriter(s). Winners are in bold type.

19TH ANNUAL (1976) GRAMMY AWARDS
Announced February 19, 1977

ALBUM OF THE YEAR
***Songs in the Key of Life* / Stevie Wonder**
Breezin' / George Benson
Chicago X / Chicago
Frampton Comes Alive! / Peter Frampton
Silk Degrees / Boz Scaggs

RECORD OF THE YEAR
"This Masquerade" / George Benson
"Afternoon Delight" / Starland Vocal Band
"Fifty Ways to Leave Your Lover" / Paul Simon
"I Write the Songs" / Barry Manilow
"If You Leave Me Now" / Chicago

SONG OF THE YEAR
"I Write the Songs" / Bruce Johnston (songwriter)
"Afternoon Delight" / Bill Danoff (songwriter)
"Breaking Up Is Hard to Do" / Neil Sedaka, Howard Greenfield (songwriter)

"This Masquerade" / Leon Russell (songwriter)
"The Wreck of the Edmund Fitzgerald" / Gordon Lightfoot (songwriter)

BEST NEW ARTIST
Starland Vocal Band
Boston
Dr. Buzzard's Original "Savannah" Band
The Brothers Johnson
Wild Cherry

BEST POP VOCAL PERFORMANCE, FEMALE
Hasten Down the Wind / **Linda Ronstadt**
Natalie / Natalie Cole
Here, There and Everywhere / Emmylou Harris
The Hissing of Summer Lawns / Joni Mitchell
"Turn the Beat Around" / Vicki Sue Robinson

BEST POP VOCAL PERFORMANCE, MALE
Songs in the Key of Life / **Stevie Wonder**
"This Masquerade" / George Benson
"The Wreck of the Edmund Fitzgerald" / Gordon Lightfoot
"You'll Never Find Another Love Like Mine" / Lou Rawls
Silk Degrees / Boz Scaggs

BEST POP VOCAL PERFORMANCE, GROUP
"If You Leave Me Now" / Chicago
"Don't Go Breaking My Heart" / Elton John and Kiki Dee
"I'd Really Love to See You Tonight" / England Dan and John Ford Coley
"Afternoon Delight" / Starland Vocal Band
"Bohemian Rhapsody" / Queen

BEST RHYTHM & BLUES SONG

"Lowdown" / Boz Scaggs, David Paich (songwriters)

"Disco Lady" / Harvey Scales, Al Vance, Don Davis (songwriters)

"Love Hangover" / Pam Sawyer, Marylin McLeod (songwriters)

"Misty Blue" / Bob Montgomery (songwriter)

"(Shake, Shake, Shake) Shake Your Booty" / H. W. Casey, Richard Finch (songwriters)

BEST RHYTHM & BLUES VOCAL PERFORMANCE, FEMALE

"Sophisticated Lady (She's a Different Lady)" / Natalie Cole

"Something He Can Feel" / Aretha Franklin

"Misty Blue" / Dorothy Moore

"Lean On Me" / Melba Moore

"Love Hangover" / Diana Ross

BEST RHYTHM & BLUES VOCAL PERFORMANCE, MALE

"I Wish" / Stevie Wonder

I Want You / Marvin Gaye

"Groovy People" / Lou Rawls

"Lowdown" / Boz Scaggs

"I Need You, You Need Me" / Joe Simon

"Disco Lady" / Johnnie Taylor

BEST RHYTHM & BLUES VOCAL PERFORMANCE, GROUP

"You Don't Have to Be a Star (To Be in My Show)" / Marilyn McCoo and Billy Davis Jr.

Gratitude / Earth, Wind and Fire

"(Shake, Shake, Shake) Shake Your Booty" / K.C. and the Sunshine Band
"Rubberband Man" / Spinners
"Play That Funky Music" / Wild Cherry

20TH ANNUAL (1977) GRAMMY AWARDS
Announced February 23, 1978

ALBUM OF THE YEAR
Rumours / **Fleetwood Mac**
Aja / Steely Dan
Hotel California / The Eagles
J.T. / James Taylor
Star Wars / John Williams conducting the London Symphony Orchestra

RECORD OF THE YEAR
"Hotel California" / The Eagles
"Blue Bayou" / Linda Ronstadt
"Don't It Make My Brown Eyes Blue" / Crystal Gayle
"Evergreen" / Barbra Streisand
"You Light Up My Life" / Debby Boone

SONG OF THE YEAR (TIE)
"Evergreen" / Barbra Streisand, Paul Williams (song-writers)
"You Light Up My Life" / Joe Brooks (songwriter)
"Don't It Make My Brown Eyes Blue" / Richard Leigh (songwriter)
"Nobody Does It Better" / Marvin Hamlisch, Carole Bayer Sager (songwriters)
"Southern Nights" / Allen Toussaint (songwriter)

BEST NEW ARTIST
Debby Boone
Stephen Bishop
Shaun Cassidy
Foreigner
Andy Gibb

BEST POP VOCAL PERFORMANCE, FEMALE
"Evergreen" / Barbra Streisand
"You Light Up My Life" / Debby Boone
"Here You Come Again" / Dolly Parton
"Blue Bayou" / Linda Ronstadt
"Nobody Does It Better" / Carly Simon

BEST POP VOCAL PERFORMANCE, MALE
"Handy Man" / James Taylor
"On and On" / Stephen Bishop
"I Just Want to Be Your Everything" / Andy Gibb
"After the Lovin'" / Engelbert Humperdinck
"When I Need You" / Leo Sayer

BEST POP VOCAL PERFORMANCE, GROUP
"How Deep Is Your Love" / Bee Gees
CSN / Crosby, Stills and Nash
Hotel California / Eagles
Rumours / Fleetwood Mac
Aja / Steely Dan

BEST RHYTHM & BLUES SONG
"You Make Me Feel Like Dancing" / Leo Sayer (songwriter)
"Best of My Love" / Maurice White, Al McKay (songwriters)
"Brickhouse" / Milan Williams, Walter Orange, Thomas

McClary, William King, Lionel Ritchie, Ronald LaPread (song-writers)

"Don't Leave Me This Way" / Kenny Gamble, Leon Huff, Carry Gilbert (songwriters)

"Easy" / Lionel Ritchie (songwriter)

BEST RHYTHM & BLUES VOCAL PERFORMANCE, FEMALE

"Don't Leave Me This Way" / Thelma Houston

"I've Got Love On My Mind" / Natalie Cole

"Break It to Me Gently" / Aretha Franklin

"I Believe You" / Dorothy Moore

"Your Love Is So Good for Me" / Diana Ross

BEST RHYTHM & BLUES VOCAL PERFORMANCE, MALE

Unmistakably Lou / **Lou Rawls**

"Got to Give It Up (Part 1)" / Marvin Gaye

"It's Just a Matter of Time" / B.B. King

"Ain't Gonna Bump No More (With No Big Fat Woman)" / Joe Tex

"A Real Mother for Ya" / Johnny "Guitar" Watson

BEST RHYTHM & BLUES VOCAL PERFORMANCE, GROUP

"Best of My Love" / Emotions

"Easy" / Commodores

"Boogie Nights" / Heatwave

"Baby Don't Change Your Mind" / Gladys Knight and the Pips

Ask Rufus / Rufus featuring Chaka Khan

21ST ANNUAL (1978) GRAMMY AWARDS
Announced February 15, 1979

ALBUM OF THE YEAR
Saturday Night Fever / Bee Gees, et al.
Even Now / Barry Manilow
Grease / John Travolta, Olivia Newton-John, et al.
Running on Empty / Jackson Browne
Some Girls / The Rolling Stones

RECORD OF THE YEAR
"Just the Way You Are" / Billy Joel
"Baker Street" / Gerry Rafferty
"Feels So Good" / Chuck Mangione
"Stayin' Alive" / Bee Gees
"You Needed Me" / Anne Murray

SONG OF THE YEAR
"Just the Way You Are" / Billy Joel (songwriter)
"Stayin' Alive" / Barry Gibb, Robin Gibb, Maurice Gibb (songwriters)
"Three Times a Lady" / Lionel Ritchie (songwriter)
"You Don't Bring Me Flowers" / Neil Diamond, Alan Bergman, Marylin Bergman (songwriters)
"You Needed Me" / Randy Goodrum (songwriter)

BEST NEW ARTIST
A Taste of Honey
The Cars
Elvis Costello
Chris Rea
Toto

BEST POP VOCAL PERFORMANCE, FEMALE
"You Needed Me" / Anne Murray
"Hopelessly Devoted to You" / Olivia Newton-John

"You Belong to Me" / Carly Simon
"You Don't Bring Me Flowers" (solo version) / Barbra Streisand
"MacArthur Park" / Donna Summer

BEST POP VOCAL PERFORMANCE, MALE
"Copacabana (At the Copa)" / Barry Manilow
Running On Empty / Jackson Browne
"Sometimes When We Touch" / Dan Hill
"Baker Street" / Gerry Rafferty
"I Just Wanna Stop" / Gino Vannelli

BEST POP VOCAL PERFORMANCE, GROUP
***Saturday Night Fever* / Bee Gees**
"Three Times a Lady" / Commodores
"Got to Get You Into My Life" / Earth, Wind and Fire
"The Closer I Get to You" / Roberta Flack and Donny Hathaway
"FM (No Static At All)" / Steely Dan

BEST RHYTHM & BLUES SONG
"Last Dance" / Paul Jabara (songwriter)
"Boogie Oogie Oogie" / Perry Kibble, Janice Johnson (songwriters)
"Dance, Dance, Dance," / Bernard Edwards, Kenny Lehman, Nile Rogers (songwriters)
"Fantasy" / Maurice White, Eddie de Barrio, Verdine White (songwriters)
"Use Ta Be My Girl" / Kenneth Gamble, Leon Huff (songwriters)

BEST RHYTHM & BLUES VOCAL PERFORMANCE, FEMALE
"Last Dance" / Donna Summer
"I Love the Nightlife" / Alicia Bridges
"Our Love" / Natalie Cole

Almighty Fire / Aretha Franklin

"I'm Every Woman" / Chaka Khan

BEST RHYTHM & BLUES VOCAL PERFORMANCE, MALE

"On Broadway" / George Benson

"Dance with Me" / Peter Brown

"I Can See Clearly Now" / Ray Charles

"Close the Door" / Teddy Pendergrass

When You Hear Lou, You've Heard It All / Lou Rawls

BEST RHYTHM & BLUES VOCAL PERFORMANCE, GROUP

All 'n All **/ Earth, Wind and Fire**

"Boogie Oogie Oogie" / A Taste of Honey

Natural High / Commodores

"Use Ta Be My Girl" / The O'Jays

"Ease On Down the Road" / Diana Ross and Michael Jackson

22ND ANNUAL (1979) GRAMMY AWARDS

Announced February 27, 1980

ALBUM OF THE YEAR

52nd Street **/ Billy Joel**

Bad Girls / Donna Summer

Breakfast in America / Supertramp

The Gambler / Kenny Rogers

Minute by Minute / Doobie Brothers

RECORD OF THE YEAR

"What a Fool Believes" / The Doobie Brothers

"After the Love Has Gone" / Earth, Wind and Fire

"The Gambler" / Kenny Rogers

"I Will Survive" / Gloria Gaynor

"You Don't Bring Me Flowers" / Barbra Streisand and Neil Diamond

SONG OF THE YEAR

"What a Fool Believes" / Kenny Loggins, Michael McDonald (songwriters)

"After the Love Has Gone" / David Foster, Jay Graydon, Bill Champlain (songwriters)

"Chuck E.'s In Love" / Rickie Lee Jones (songwriter)

"Honesty" / Billy Joel (songwriter)

"I Will Survive" / Dino Fekaris, Freddie Perren (songwriters)

"Minute by Minute" / Michael McDonald, Lester Abrams (songwriters)

"Reunited" / Dino Fekaris, Freddie Perren (songwriters)

"She Believes in Me" / Steve Gibb (songwriter)

BEST NEW ARTIST

Rickie Lee Jones

The Blues Brothers

Dire Straits

The Knack

Robin Williams

BEST POP VOCAL PERFORMANCE, FEMALE

"I'll Never Love This Way Again" / Dionne Warwick

"I Will Survive" / Gloria Gaynor

"Chuck E.'s In Love" / Rickie Lee Jones

"Don't Cry Out Loud" / Melissa Manchester

Bad Girls / Donna Summer

BEST POP VOCAL PERFORMANCE, MALE
52nd Street / **Billy Joel**
"Sad Eyes" / Robert John

"She Believes in Me" / Kenny Rogers

"Da Ya Think I'm Sexy?" / Rod Stewart

"Up On the Roof" / James Taylor

BEST ROCK VOCAL PERFORMANCE, FEMALE (NEW CATEGORY)
"Hot Stuff" / Donna Summer
"Survivor" / Cindy Bullens

"Last Chance Texaco" / Rickie Lee Jones

"You're Gonna Get What's Comin' " / Bonnie Raitt

"Vengeance" / Carly Simon

TNT / Tanya Tucker

BEST ROCK VOCAL PERFORMANCE, MALE (NEW CATEGORY)
"Gotta Serve Somebody" / Bob Dylan
"Is She Really Going Out with Him" / Joe Jackson

"Bad Case of Loving You (Doctor, Doctor)" / Robert Palmer

"Blondes (Have More Fun)" / Rod Stewart

"Dancin' Fool" / Frank Zappa

BEST ROCK VOCAL PERFORMANCE, GROUP (NEW CATEGORY)
"Heartache Tonight" / Eagles
Briefcase Full of Blues / The Blues Brothers

Candy-O / The Cars

"Sultans of Swing" / Dire Straits

"My Sharona" / The Knack

Cornerstone / Styx

BEST RHYTHM & BLUES SONG
"After the Love Has Gone" / David Foster, Jay Graydon, Bill Champlain (songwriters)
"Ain't No Stoppin' Us Now" / Gene McFadden, John Whitehead, Jerry Cohen (songwriters)
"Déjà Vu" / Isaac Hayes, Adrienne Anderson (songwriters)
"Reunited" / Dino Ferkaris, Freddie Perren (songwriters)
"We Are Family" / Nile Rogers, Bernard Edwards (songwriters)

BEST RHYTHM & BLUES VOCAL PERFORMANCE, FEMALE
"Déjà Vu" / Dionne Warwick
I Love You So / Natalie Cole
Minnie / Minnie Riperton
"Knock On Wood" / Amii Stewart
"Dim All the Lights" / Donna Summer
"Ring My Bell" / Anita Ward

BEST RHYTHM & BLUES VOCAL PERFORMANCE, MALE
"Don't Stop 'Til You Get Enough" / Michael Jackson
"Love Ballad" / George Benson
"Some Enchanted Evening" / Ray Charles
"Don't Let Go" / Isaac Hayes
"Mama Can't Buy You Love" / Elton John
"Cruisin'" / Smokey Robinson

BEST RHYTHM & BLUES VOCAL PERFORMANCE, GROUP
"After the Love Has Gone" / Earth, Wind and Fire
Midnight Magic / Commodores
"Ain't No Stoppin' Us Now" / McFadden and Whitehead

"Reunited" / Peaches and Herb
"We Are Family" / Sister Sledge

BEST DISCO RECORDING (NEW CATEGORY)
"I Will Survive" / Gloria Gaynor
"Boogie Wonderland" / Earth, Wind and Fire
Bad Girls / Donna Summer
"Da Ya Think I'm Sexy?" / Rod Stewart
"Don't Stop 'Til You Get Enough" / Michael Jackson

Artists passed over for "Best New Artist" nominations, 1976–79: Prince, Talking Heads, Bob Marley, Kate Bush, Peter Gabriel, XTC, Joe Jackson, The Clash, Tom Petty, Chic, Al Jarreau, and Warren Zevon.

Rock's Front Page:

Rolling Stone cover stories, 1976–79

1976

Jefferson Starship

Rolling Thunder Revue

Pat Boone

David Bowie

San Francisco Scene

Donny Osmond

Mary Hartman, Mary Hartman

All the President's Men

Peter Frampton

Santana

Marlon Brando

Jimmy Carter

Paul McCartney

Paul Simon

The Beatles

Jack Ford

Bob Marley

Aerosmith

Doonesbury

Neil Diamond

Elton John

Richard Avedon portraits

Brian Wilson

Janis Joplin

Linda Ronstadt

Jackson Browne
Maurice Sendak

1977
Rod Stewart
Jeff Bridges
Peter Frampton
Boz Scaggs
Princess Caroline
Fleetwood Mac
Lily Tomlin
Hall and Oates
Mark Fidrych
White House "whiz kids"
Crosby, Stills and Nash
Robert De Niro
Diane Keaton
Bee Gees
Heart
Diana Ross
Star Wars
O.J. Simpson
Elvis Presley
Bella Abzug
Sex Pistols
Ron Wood
Pete Townshend
Steve Martin
Tenth-anniversary edition
James Taylor and Linda Ronstadt

1978

Fleetwood Mac
Bob Dylan
Doonesbury
Rita Coolidge and Kris Kristofferson
Jane Fonda
Donna Summer
Brooke Shields
Bee Gees
Muhammad Ali
Jefferson Starship
Carly Simon
John Travolta
Mick Jagger
Willie Nelson
Patti Smith
John Belushi
Bruce Springsteen
Mick Jagger and Keith Richards
Gary Busey
The Who
Linda Ronstadt
Gilda Radner
Bob Dylan
Linda Ronstadt, Gilda Radner, and Steve Martin
Cheech and Chong

1979

Richard Dreyfuss
The Cars
Neil Young
The Blues Brothers
Ted Nugent

Johnny Carson
Michael Douglas
The Village People
Richard Pryor
Bee Gees
John Voigt
Cheap Trick
Blondie
Paul McCartney
Joni Mitchell
Rickie Lee Jones
Robin Williams
James Taylor
The Doobie Brothers
Jimmy Buffet
Sissy Spacek
Martin Sheen
MUSE Concerts
The Eagles
Bette Midler

Bibliography

Allen, Woody. *The Complete Prose of Woody Allen.* New York: Random House, 1991.

Bangs, Lester. *Psychotic Reactions and Carburetor Dung.* New York: Vintage, 1988.

Bronson, Fred. *The Billboard Book of Number One Hits.* New York: Billboard Publications, 1985.

Christgau, Robert. *Rock Albums of the '70s: A Critical Guide.* New York: Da Capo Press, 1990.

Crampton, Luke, and Dafydd Rees. *DK Encyclopedia of Rock Stars.* New York: DK Publishing, Inc., 1996.

Dannen, Fredric. *Hit Men: Power Brokers and Fast Money Inside the Music Business.* New York: Random House, 1990.

DeCurtis, Anthony, James Henke, and Holly George-Warren, eds. *The Rolling Stone Illustrated History of Rock and Roll.* New York: Random House, 1992.

Feather, Leonard, and Ira Gitler. *The Encyclopedia of Jazz in the '70s.* New York: Horizon Press, 1976.

Flanagan, Bill. *Written in My Soul: Conversations with Rock's Great Songwriters.* Chicago: Contemporary Books, Inc., 1986.

George, Nelson. *The Death of Rhythm and Blues.* New York: Dutton, 1989.

Giuliano, Geoffrey. *Blackbird: The Life and Times of Paul McCartney.* Toronto: McGraw-Hill Ryerson, 1991.

Guralnick, Peter. *Sweet Soul Music: Rhythm and Blues and the Southern Dream of Freedom.* New York: Harper and Row, 1986.

Hall, Ron. *The Chum Chart Book.* Toronto: Stardust, 1984.

Jackson, Rick. *Encyclopedia of Canadian Rock, Pop and Folk.* Kingston: Quarry Publications, 1994.

Jancik, Wayne. *The Billboard Book of One-Hit Wonders.* New York: Billboard Publications, 1990.

Jasper, Tony. *Simply Pop.* London: Queen Tune Press, 1975.

Kael, Pauline. *For Keeps: Thirty Years at the Movies.* New York: Dutton, 1994.

Kahn, Ashley, Holly George-Warren, and Shawn Dahl, eds. *The Seventies.* New York: Little, Brown and Company, 1998.

Kennedy, Pagan. *Platforms: A Microwaved Cultural Chronicle of the 1970s.* New York: St. Martin's, 1994.

Knobler, Peter, and Greg Mitchell, eds. *Very Seventies: A Cultural History of the 1970s from the Pages of Crawdaddy.* New York: Fireside, 1995.

Kohut, Joe, and John J. Kohut. *Rock Talk: The Great Rock and Roll Quote Book.* Boston: Faber and Faber, 1994.

Larkin, Colin. *The Virgin Encyclopedia of Seventies Music.* London: Muze UK Ltd, 1997.

Luftig, Stacy, ed. *The Paul Simon Companion.* New York: Schirmer Books, 1997.

Marsh, Dave. *The Heart of Rock and Soul: The 1001 Greatest Singles Ever Made.* New York: New American Library, 1989.

Nite, Norm N. *Rock on Almanac: The First Four Decades of Rock 'n' Roll.* New York: Harper and Row, 1989.

O'Neil, Thomas. *The Grammys.* New York: Perigee, 1999.

O'Rourke, P.J. *Age and Guile Beat Youth, Innocence, and a Bad Haircut.* Toronto: Random House, 1995.

Palmer, Robert. *Rock and Roll: An Unruly History.* New York: Harmony Books, 1995.

Romanowski, Patricia, and Holly George-Warren, eds. *The New Rolling Stone Encyclopedia of Rock and Roll.* New York: Fireside, 1995.

Russell, Tom, and Sylvia Tyson, eds. *And Then I Wrote: The Songwriter Speaks.* Vancouver: Arsenal Pulp Press, 1995.

Schipper, Henry. *Broken Record: The Inside Story of the Grammy Awards.* New York: Birch Lane Press, 1992.

Slansky, Paul. *The Clothes Have No Emperor: A Chronicle of the American '80s*. New York: Simon and Schuster, 1989.

Smith, Joe. *Off the Record: An Oral History of Popular Music*. New York: Warner, 1988.

Sweet, Brian. *Reelin' in the Years*. London: Omnibus Press, 1994.

Swenson, John. *Stevie Wonder*. London: Plexus, 1976.

Tobler, John. *This Day in Rock: Day by Day Record of Rock's Biggest News Stories*. London: Carlton, 1993.

Waldron, Vince. *Classic Sitcoms: A Celebration of the Best of Prime-Time Comedy*. New York: Macmillan, 1987.

Whitburn, Joel. *Billboard Hot 100 Charts: The Seventies*. Menomonee Falls, WI: Record Research, 1990.

Whitburn, Joel. *The Billboard Book of Top 40 Hits*. New York: Billboard Publications, 1989.

Whitburn, Joel. *Bubbling Under the Hot 100 1959–1985*. Menomonee Falls, WI: Record Research, 1992.

Whitburn, Joel. *Top Pop Albums 1955–1996*. Menomonee Falls, WI: Record Research, 1996.

Whitburn, Joel. *Top Pop Singles 1955–1996*. Menomonee Falls, WI: Record Research, 1997.

White, Adam. *The Billboard Book of Gold and Platinum Records*. New York: Billboard Publications, 1990.

White, Timothy. *Catch a Fire: The Life of Bob Marley.* New York: Henry Holt, 1989.

Zappa, Frank, with Peter Occhiogrosso. *The Real Frank Zappa Book.* New York: Poseidon Press, 1989.

Artist Index